FUN FACTS
CRAZY STORIES
& ODD AND UNUSUAL
TRIVIA FACTS!

Contents

Introduction

This book is full of fun, fascinating, and strange facts about the United States, exploring its history, culture, people, and landmarks! We also uncover some curious stories and interesting facts from around the world!

You'll discover a range of weird, wacky, and unbelievable facts and stories that will pique your curiosity and entertain you for hours! We go from the hilarious to the bizarre, so this book should have something for everyone. Whether you're a history buff, a trivia enthusiast, or simply enjoy a good laugh, this book should satisfy your hunger for knowledge and entertainment. So what are you waiting for? Discover the wild and wacky world of *Fun Facts, Crazy Stories, & Odd and Unusual Trivia Facts!*

Chapter 1

Curious facts and stories about the human body

- The human eye can distinguish over 10 million different colors, making it one of the most complex visual systems in the animal kingdom.

- The human body contains enough water to fill a 50-liter (13-gallon) tank.

- The human body contains enough calcium to make about 1,200 tubes of toothpaste.

- The human body contains enough iron to make a 3-inch nail.

- The human body contains enough potassium to fire a toy cannon.

- The female egg is the largest cell in the human body, and the smallest is the male sperm.

- The average person walks the equivalent of three times around the world in a lifetime.

- An average person produces enough saliva throughout their life to fill two swimming pools.

- There are about 100,000 hairs on an average person's heads.

- The human heart pumps enough blood in a single day to fill a tanker truck.

- The human brain is made up of about 75% water.

- The human body has enough bones to make up about 20% of an adult's body weight.

- The human nose can distinguish over 1 trillion different scents, which makes it one of the most advanced in the animal kingdom.

- The human heart can pump blood to the body at a rate of up to 2,000 gallons per day.

- The human brain can generate more electrical impulses daily than all the telephones in the world combined.

- The human body contains enough phosphorus to make 2,200 matchheads.

- The human body has enough sulfur to kill all the fleas on an average dog.

- The human body is capable of healing itself. The skin, for example, can regenerate itself in as little as two weeks.

- The human body can repair itself after physical injuries, such as cuts, bruises, and broken bones.

- The human body has the ability to adapt to various environments and conditions. For example, humans living at high altitudes have developed larger lungs to help them breathe in thin air.

- The human body can produce its own vitamin D when the skin sees enough sunlight.

- The human body has enough fat to make seven bars of soap, but it is also capable of burning fat for energy.

- The human body is made up of about 60% water, which is essential for many of the body's functions.

- The human body contains over 600 muscles, which are responsible for movement and support.

- The human body can detect temperature changes and adjust itself to maintain a consistent internal temperature.

- The human body can filter out harmful substances from the bloodstream through the liver and kidneys.

- The human body can repair damaged DNA, which is essential for maintaining the integrity of our genetic material.

- There have been rare cases of people surviving without a functioning heart. These individuals have a condition called hypoplastic left heart syndrome, where the left side of the heart is severely underdeveloped. They are able to survive by using a combination of medications and artificial support systems to perform the functions of the heart.

- Some people can survive severe blood loss because their bodies are able to generate new blood cells to replace the ones lost. This process is called hematopoiesis, and it occurs in the bone marrow.

- There have been cases of people who have survived after falling from extremely high altitudes. In 1972, Vesna Vulovic, a flight attendant, survived a fall from an altitude of 33,000 feet (10,000 meters) when the plane she was on exploded in mid-air. She fell unconscious during the fall and was found alive in the wreckage.

- Some people can withstand extremely cold temperatures because their bodies can generate extra heat to keep themselves warm. This is known as non-shivering thermogenesis, and it occurs when the body breaks down stored fats and sugars to generate heat.

- Some people can survive without a functioning brain or with only a small portion of their brain remaining. These individuals have a condition called hydrocephalus, in which the brain is damaged or not fully developed. They are able to survive because the remaining portion of the brain is able to take over the functions of the damaged portion.

- In 2014, a man in China had a five-inch nail removed from his head after it had been lodged there for 26 years! The nail had been accidentally stuck in his head while working as a carpenter, and he never sought medical attention.

- In 2017, surgeons at a hospital in India removed a four-pound hairball from a teenager's stomach. The hairball, known as a trichobezoar, was causing the teenager to feel nauseous and lose weight.

- In 2019, a woman in the UK gave birth to naturally-conceived quadruplets, a rare occurrence that has a probability of about 1 in 15 million.

- In 2018, a man in the United States had a 132-pound tumor removed from his abdomen. The tumor had been growing for over 20 years and was thought to be one of the largest tumors ever recorded.

- In 2020, a woman in the United States gave birth to a baby with a fully-formed tooth. This is a rare occurrence, with only about 1 in 2,000 babies being born with a tooth.

- The human body contains over 600 skeletal muscles, which make up about 40% of a person's body weight.

- The human body has over 100,000 miles of blood vessels, which is enough to circle the Earth four times.

- The human body has over 60,000 miles of nerves, which is enough to stretch from New York to Los Angeles six times.

- The human body has over 300 bones at birth, but by the time a person reaches adulthood, some of the bones have joined together, leaving 206 bones in the adult body.

- The human body has over 8,000 taste buds responsible for detecting sweet, sour, salty, and bitter flavors.

- The human body has a natural defense system known as the "acid mantle," which helps to protect the skin from any harmful bacteria and other external threats it is exposed to.

- The human body has a built-in cooling system known as "perspiration," which helps to regulate body temperature and prevent overheating.

- The human body has a natural defense system known as the "immune system," which helps to protect the body from diseases and infections.

Chapter 2

Fun facts about American presidents

- The Whig Party, along with the Democratic Party, was one of two major political parties in the United States during the mid-19th century. The party's name, "Whig," was a reference to the British political party with the same name that had opposed the absolute rule of monarchs in the 18th century. Millard Fillmore was the last president who was a member of the Whig party.

- The first president to ever be photographed was John Quincy Adams.

- The first president being born a United States citizen was Martin Van Buren. All previous presidents had been born British.

- In 1868, President Andrew Johnson was impeached by the U.S. House of Representatives for "high crimes and misdemeanors." He was the first President to be impeached, and he narrowly avoided being removed from office by the Senate.

- According to legend, there is a White House's resident ghost, known as the "Ghost of the White House". The ghost is the spirit of Abigail Adams, President John Adams's wife and the mother of President John Quincy Adams. Abigail Adams is said to haunt the White House because she was unhappy with how her husband treated her and concerned about the country's future. Some people claim to have seen or heard the ghost in various parts of the White House, and others claim to have felt its presence. While the story of the Ghost of the White House is difficult to verify, it is an enduring legend that has captured people's imaginations for many years.

- James Monroe was the last president to have served in the Revolutionary War.

- The first ever African American President of the United States, Barack Obama, was elected in 2009 and served two terms in office.

- The first president ever to ride on a train was Andrew Jackson.

- George Washington's teeth were not created out of wood. However, he did have several sets of dentures made from materials such as animal teeth and ivory, but not wood.

- William Henry Harrison gave the absolute longest inaugural speech in history, lasting over two hours. He also had the shortest presidency, serving only 31 days before dying of pneumonia.

- The first American vice president to assume the presidency upon the president's death was John Tyler. He was also the only president to have been a member of both the Democratic and the Whig parties.

- James K. Polk was the first President of the United States to have his photograph taken while in office.

- Zachary Taylor was the second American president to die in office, after only serving 16 months.

- The tradition of decorating Christmas trees was not as widespread in America in the 19th century as it is today, so Franklin Pierce, the 14th serving President of the United States, was the first president ever to have a Christmas tree in the White House.

- The only president who never married was James Buchanan.

- George Washington had a set of false teeth made from a combination of materials, including animal teeth and ivory. Contrary to popular belief, they were not made out of wood.

- Abraham Lincoln was known for his tall and lanky stature, but he was also known to be prone to depression and struggled with mental health issues throughout his life.

- James Garfield, the 20th serving president of the United States, was a talented linguist and was fluent in Greek, Latin, and several modern languages. He was also a skilled writer and was the first president to have a published poem.

- Theodore Roosevelt, the 26th president, was an avid outdoorsman and conservationist. He was known for his love of hunting and was the first president to go on a safari, during which he collected specimens for the Smithsonian Institution.

- John F. Kennedy, the 35th president, was a Harvard graduate and a published author. He wrote a Pulitzer Prize-winning book called "Profiles in Courage," which highlighted the acts of bravery and integrity of various American politicians.

- Lyndon B. Johnson, the 36th president, was known for his strong personality and aggressive negotiating style. He was also known to have a volatile temper and was prone to outbursts of anger.

- Richard Nixon, the 37th president, was the first and only president to resign from office. He resigned in 1974 amid the Watergate scandal, in which it was revealed that he had ordered the break-in at the Democratic National Committee headquarters.

- Gerald Ford, the 38th president, was the first and only president to have served as both vice president and president without ever being elected to either office. He became vice president after Spiro Agnew resigned and became president after Nixon resigned.

- Jimmy Carter, the 39th president, was a peanut farmer and a naval officer before entering politics. He was also the first president to be born in a hospital.

- Ronald Reagan, the 40th president, was an actor before entering politics. He appeared in over 50 films and television shows, including "Kings Row" and "Death Valley Days."

- George H. W. Bush, the 41st serving president, was a World War II veteran and a successful businessman before entering politics. He was also the first president ever to have a bachelor's degree in business administration.

- Bill Clinton, the 42nd president, was a Rhodes Scholar and a talented saxophonist. He had played the saxophone on "The Arsenio Hall Show" and several other television appearances.

- George W. Bush, the 43rd president, was a pilot in the Texas Air National Guard and a successful businessman before entering politics. He was also the first American president to have an MBA degree.

- Barack Obama, the 44th president, was a community organizer and a constitutional law professor before entering politics. He was additionally the first president to have a degree in political science.

- Donald Trump, the 45th president, was a real estate developer and a television personality before entering politics. He was additionally the first president to have a background in entertainment.

- John F. Kennedy and Abraham Lincoln both had strange coincidences surrounding their assassinations. Lincoln was assassinated on Good Friday, and Kennedy was assassinated on the anniversary of Lincoln's assassination.

- Theodore Roosevelt was the first American president to travel outside the United States while in office, and he made several trips to Latin America and Europe.

- John F. Kennedy was the first American president to hold a live televised press conference and held a total of 177 such conferences during his time in office.

- George Washington was known for his strong leadership and integrity, but he also had a mischievous side. As a young man, he once chopped down his father's prized cherry tree and then famously admitted to the deed when confronted, saying, "I cannot tell a lie." While likely not true, this story has become a part of Washington's legacy and is often taught to children as a lesson in honesty.

Chapter 3

Unusual facts and stories about American inventors

- The "Franklin stove" was invented to make fireplace fires more efficient, and was named after Benjamin Franklin, who is said to have invented it. However, in reality, Franklin did not invent the stove. Rather, he made improvements to an existing design. Despite this, the stove became known as the Franklin stove, and it is still known by that name today.

- Believe it or not, Thomas Edison was once electrocuted by one of his own inventions, a machine designed to administer electric shocks as a form of medical treatment.

- The first American patent for a steamboat was granted to John Fitch in 1791. Fitch's steamboat was able to travel at a speed of about 4 miles per hour, faster than any other watercraft of the time, and it was also the first boat to be powered by an engine.

- The inventor of the telephone, Alexander Graham Bell, was once accidentally electrocuted by his own device when he dropped it in a bathtub.

- The first American patent for a cotton gin, which stands for "cotton engine", was granted to Eli Whitney in 1794. This machine quickly and easily separates cotton fibers from their seeds, allowing for much more efficient cotton production.

- The Wright brothers, Orville and Wilbur, were not the first to invent the airplane, but they were the first to develop a successful, practical aircraft that could be controlled by the pilot.

- A popular toy consisting of a coiled spring, called the Slinky, was invented by chance when its creator, Richard James, accidentally knocked a spring off a table and watched it "walk" away.

- The first American patent for a GPS device was granted to Roger L. Easton in 1973. He later received the National Medal of Technology for his work in this field.

- Thomas Edison was a prolific inventor who held over 1,000 patents, including the light bulb, the phonograph, and the motion picture camera.

- The microwave oven was invented by chance when Percy Spencer, an engineer at Raytheon, discovered that microwaves emitted from a radar magnetron could cook food when he accidentally melted a candy bar in his pocket while working on radar equipment.

- Robert Goddard, the father of modern rocketry, was once ridiculed by the New York Times for his ideas about space travel. However, his work eventually led to the development of the first successful rocket.

- The first American patent for a typewriter was granted to

Christopher Sholes in 1868. However, Sholes sold the rights to his invention to the Remington Arms Company, a manufacturer of guns and sewing machines. This company began mass-producing the new machine and marketing it as the Remington No. 1, and it became the first commercially successful typewriter.

- During the Great Depression, the game Monopoly was invented by Charles Darrow to pass the time.

- Abraham Karem was an Iraqi-born Jewish engineer who emigrated to the U.S. in the 1970s. To prove the potential of his drone invention, Karem decided to build a full-scale prototype of his drone and fly it on the National Mall in Washington, D.C. The drone attracted a lot of attention, and eventually, the government began funding his research, leading to the issuance of the first American patent for a drone to Abraham Karem in 1990.

- The post-it note was invented by 3M engineer Art Fry, who came up with the idea of using a weak adhesive to stick notes to paper after his bookmark kept falling out of his hymnal at church.

- The first American patent for a sewing machine was granted to Elias Howe in 1846. Interestingly, Howe struggled to make a profit from his invention due to a lack of initial interest and the infringement of his patent by other manufacturers. However, with the help of a lawyer, he was able to sue these manufacturers and eventually receive royalties for his invention. In addition, he not only revolutionized the industry with his mechanical invention but also with legal strategies, as he was among the first inventors to deal with patent infringement lawsuits and the creation of the first license agreement.

- The disposable razor was invented by King Gillette, who thought of using a razor with a disposable blade after being frustrated with the difficulty of sharpening traditional razors.

- The chocolate chip cookie was invented by Ruth Wakefield, who ran the Toll House Inn in Massachusetts and added chopped-up bits of chocolate to her cookie dough on a whim.

- The first American patent for a laser was granted to Theodore Maiman in 1960. Initially, many scientists and experts did not believe that Maiman's invention would work. To prove them wrong, Maiman set up his laser in a lab and invited the scientists to come and see it in action. When they arrived, Maiman turned on the laser and aimed it at a target across the room. To the surprise of everyone present, the laser beam shot across the room and drilled a small hole in the target. The scientists were amazed, and many of them immediately recognized the potential of Maiman's invention. This marked the beginning of widespread research and development in laser technology.

- The telephone was originally intended to be a device for transmitting multiple telegraph messages at once, but Alexander Graham Bell eventually realized its potential as a means of communication.

- The pacemaker was invented by Wilson Greatbatch, who attempted to build a device for recording heart sounds but accidentally left a resistor out of the circuit, causing the device to emit regular electrical pulses.

- The first American patent for a search engine was granted to Larry Page and Sergey Brin in 1998. It resulted from a research project they worked on while studying at Stanford University. The project was not initially intended to be a search engine but rather a way for them to study the structure of the web. However, page and Brin were convinced it could be developed into something more, so they continued to work on the project during their spare time. Eventually, they decided to turn their research into a company, which they named Google. The patent was granted to them for the PageRank algorithm, which is the foundation of their search engine.

- The Slinky was initially a commercial failure when it was released, but it became a popular toy after being featured on the TV show "The Philadelphia Story."

- The Super Soaker, a popular water gun toy, was invented by Lonnie Johnson, a nuclear engineer working on a heat pump when he accidentally sprayed water across the room.

- The Frisbee was originally a pie tin produced by the Frisbie Baking Company. College students in Connecticut would toss the empty tins to each other as a form of entertainment.

- The zipper was invented by Whitcomb Judson, and it was not initially well received. Judson's zipper was originally called the "Clasp Locker" and later version the "Separable Fastener", but it wasn't until B.F Goodrich used it on rubber boots, calling it "zipper" in 1923 that it began to gain some popularity. It took some time for the zipper to become widely accepted and adopted in various industries, such as clothing, bags, and even airplanes. Today, zippers are an essential part of our everyday life, and it's hard to imagine a world without them, but at the time of its invention, it was not well received.

- The first American patent for a barcode was granted to Norman Woodland and Bernard Silver in 1952. They came up with the idea while they were students at Drexel Institute of Technology in Philadelphia, working on a class project to create a system automatically tracking inventory in a grocery store. However, after they graduated, they struggled to find a company that was interested in their invention. It wasn't until the 1960s, when the first barcode scanner was developed, that their invention began to gain traction. Today, barcodes are used everywhere, but at the time of their invention, it was not well received.

- The Barbie doll was invented by Ruth Handler, who was inspired by a German doll called Lilli and wanted to create a similar doll for her daughter.

- The television was invented by Philo Farnsworth, who came up with the idea while plowing a potato field and visualizing a way to transmit pictures through the air.

- The first American patent for a computer was granted to John Atanasoff and Clifford Berry in 1973. However, their invention, the Atanasoff-Berry Computer (ABC), was not widely recognized or acknowledged at the time it was built. They began working on the ABC in the late 1930s, but it wasn't until the 1970s, and the invention of the first microprocessors, that the ABC began to gain recognition. Even then, the patent was disputed and not officially granted till 1973.

- The popsicle was invented by chance by an 11-year-old boy named Frank Epperson, who left a mixture of powdered soda and water on his porch with a stirring stick, and it froze overnight.

- The toilet paper roll was invented by Seth Wheeler, who patented the idea of perforating the paper and attaching it to a roll in 1891.

- Philo Farnsworth, an American inventor, was granted the first patent for television in 1927. He was just a teenager, working on his family's farm in Idaho, plowing a field when he had a vision of using a series of scanning lines to transmit images electronically. He later developed the concept further and filed for a patent in 1927. However, a patent dispute with RCA, a major player in the radio industry at the time, went on for years, arguing that Farnsworth's invention was not original and that other inventors had come up with similar ideas. In the end, Farnsworth's patent was upheld, and he is now widely recognized as the "father of television." However, despite the patent dispute, Farnsworth never became wealthy from his invention and died in 1971, relatively unknown and in poverty.

- Johan Vaaler, a Norwegian inventor, is credited with inventing the paperclip in 1899. However, the design of the modern paperclip that we know today was not actually created by Vaaler, but rather by a British man named George W. McGill in 1901. The story of Vaaler and the paperclip is often cited as an example of how ideas and inventions are often built upon and improved upon by others.

- The first American patent for a 3D printer was granted to Chuck Hull in 1986. He originally created the 3D printer to make small, plastic figurines for his daughter's diorama school project. However, he only realized his invention's potential impact on manufacturing and production afterwards.

- The hula hoop was invented by Arthur K, and it became a big fad across America in 1958.

- The trampoline was invented by George Nissen, a gymnast inspired by watching trapeze artists bounce on safety nets.

- The printing press was invented by Johannes Gutenberg, who developed a system for printing books using movable type.

- Thomas Edison, known as the "Wizard of Menlo Park," was granted the first American patent for a phonograph in 1877. During its early development, he would test the machine by recording himself singing nursery rhymes to his children. His family would often joke that they never wanted to hear "Mary Had a Little Lamb" again because they had heard it so many times during the testing phase.

- Jacques Cousteau and Emile Gagnan invented the scuba diving regulator, a device allowing divers to breathe underwater.

- The drive-through window was invented by Bank of America, which installed the first one at a branch in California in the 1950s to allow customers to make deposits without leaving their cars.

- The first American patent for a personal computer was granted to Adam Osborne in 1981. When he first introduced his portable computer, the Osborne 1, at a trade show in 1981, it generated so much excitement that people lined up to place orders on the spot. Unfortunately, Osborne made the mistake of announcing the development of his next computer, the Osborne Executive, before the Osborne 1 had even begun shipping. As a result, many people canceled their orders for the Osborne 1, thinking that a better model was on the way. This resulted in the Osborne company going out of business within a year.

- The stapler was invented by George W. McGill, who received a patent for the device in 1866.

- John Lee Love invented the pencil sharpener and developed a portable version of the device in 1897.

- Frederick McKinley Jones, an American inventor and business-man was granted the first American patent for a refrigerated truck in 1935. The first test run of this truck was a disaster, the ice cream melted, and the milk spoiled. But Jones did not give up. Instead, he worked on improving the design and finally succeeded. He went on to patent more than 60 inventions related to refrigeration and air conditioning.

- When Thomas Edison first demonstrated the phonograph to a group of friends, he recorded himself reciting "Mary had a little lamb" and then played it back. His friends were convinced that it was a trick and that there was someone hiding behind the machine or in the room, they did not believe that a machine could record and play back sound.

- The word "umbrella" comes from the Latin word for "shade", and the umbrella was originally invented to protect oneself from the sun.

- The electric guitar was invented by Les Paul, who developed the first solid-body electric guitar in 1941.

- Oliver Evans is the inventor of the refrigerator, and he received a patent for the first vapor-compression refrigeration machine in 1805. Oliver Evans was an inventor who often struggled to market his invention to the industry. His invention of the refrigeration machine was no different. It was not until he found a way to apply it to making ice cream that the machine became popular. He went door to door to visit ice cream makers and demonstrated the benefits of his refrigeration machine to them.

- The lawn mower was invented by Edwin Budding, who developed the first manual lawn mower in 1830. When he first presented his lawn mower to a group of potential investors, they were unimpressed and couldn't see the potential for it, as at that time, the lawns were kept short by grazing sheep. They thought it was a ridiculous idea and didn't invest in it. So Edwin had to find a different way to market his invention. He discovered that the lawn mower was perfect for maintaining the sports fields like cricket and soccer. The mower was able to keep the fields in excellent condition, which is how the first lawn mower was successfully marketed.

- The first American patent for a solar cell was granted to Russell Ohl in 1941. He was not initially interested in solar power but was a radio engineer designing a better crystal detector for radios.

During his work, he discovered that certain types of semiconductor materials produced an electrical current when exposed to light. He realized the potential of this discovery for creating a new kind of power source and began experimenting with solar cells. Despite initial skepticism from the industry, Ohl persisted in his research and eventually was granted the first American patent for a solar cell. This was the starting point of the modern solar cell industry.

- Benjamin Franklin was not only a founding father and scientist but also an inventor. He is credited with inventing the lightning rod, bifocal glasses, and the Franklin stove.

- Thomas Edison, often considered the greatest inventor in American history, was responsible for developing the phonograph, the motion picture camera, and the incandescent light bulb.

- The first American patent for radio was granted to Guglielmo Marconi in 1896. However, it was later invalidated in 1904 due to prior art by Nikola Tesla and others. The patent office had previously rejected Tesla's patent application for radio because they didn't believe radio waves existed. This became a humorous incident in the history of radio communication.

- George Westinghouse, an inventor and industrialist, developed the air brake system for trains, which significantly improved rail transportation safety.

- The first American patent for a cell phone was granted to Martin Cooper in 1973. When Cooper made the first public mobile phone call in front of the press on April 3, 1973, he called his rival at Bell Labs, Joel Engel, to rub it in that Motorola had beaten them to the punch. Engel answered the call, and Cooper famously said, "Joel, I'm calling you from a mobile phone, a real mobile phone, a cellular phone."

- Alexander Graham Bell, who was the inventor of the telephone, was also a teacher of the deaf and worked extensively on improving the education and communication of deaf individuals.

- The first American patent for an airplane was granted to the Wright brothers in 1906. They were not only brilliant inventors and engineers but also shrewd businesspeople. They were very protective of their patent and had a reputation for aggressively pursuing and suing any company or individual they believed was infringing on their patent. This gave them the nickname "The Flying Lawyers", as they spent almost as much time in court as they did in the air.

Chapter 4

Fun facts about American scientists

- George Washington Carver, an agricultural scientist, developed hundreds of products containing peanuts, sweet potatoes, and other crops grown by southern farmers.

- Marie Curie was the first woman to receive a Nobel Prize, and she was also the first person to receive two Nobel Prizes in different fields. She made pioneering contributions to the fields of physics and chemistry, including the discovery of radium and polonium.

- Albert Einstein is known for his theory of relativity and his equation E=mc^2, which describes the relationship between energy and mass.

- Robert Oppenheimer was a theoretical physicist who played a crucial role in developing the first nuclear weapon.

- Neil Armstrong was the first of human kind to walk on the moon. He did this as part of the Apollo 11 mission in 1969.

- Jane Goodall is a primatologist and anthropologist known for her work studying chimpanzees in Tanzania. However, when she first arrived at Gombe Stream National Park in 1960, she had no formal training in anthropology or primatology. She was simply a young woman with a love of animals and a passion for studying them. Because of her lack of formal training, her methods were considered unorthodox, causing some scientists to dismiss her work as unscientific. However, her persistence and dedication paid off, and she gathered a wealth of knowledge about chimpanzees and their behavior.

- Stephen Hawking was a cosmologist and theoretical physicist, and he made major contributions to our understanding of black holes and the understanding of the origins of the universe.

- Rosalind Franklin was a biophysicist and x-ray crystallographer who contributed significantly to the understanding of DNA structure.

- Benjamin Franklin once flew a kite during a thunderstorm to prove that lightning was a form of electricity.

- Marie Curie died from complications related to radiation exposure, which she had been exposed to while working with radioactive materials.

- Albert Einstein's theory of relativity was initially met with skepticism, but it was eventually proven correct through various experiments.

- Robert Oppenheimer was once quoted as saying, "I am become death, the destroyer of worlds," right after he witnessed the first successful test of a nuclear weapon.

- Neil Armstrong's first words upon stepping foot on the moon are known as "That's one small step for man, one giant leap for mankind," which were misquoted due to a technical glitch in the audio transmission. The quote was supposed to be, "That's one small step for a man, one giant leap for mankind."

- Jane Goodall discovered that chimpanzees use tools, a behavior that was previously thought to be exclusive to humans.

- One time Stephen Hawking threw a party for time travelers, but no one showed up. He sent out invitations after the party had already taken place in the hopes that anyone from the future who could travel through time would be able to attend.

- Grace Hopper was known for popularizing the term "debugging" after she found an actual bug in a computer she was working on.

- Lise Meitner was a physicist who made significant contributions to the understanding of nuclear fission. Still, she was not included in the Nobel Prize for this discovery because she was a woman.

- Edward Teller was a nuclear physicist who played a vital role in developing the hydrogen bomb, but he is also known for his controversial role in the blacklisting of fellow scientist Robert Oppenheimer.

- Linus Pauling was a chemist who won two Nobel Prizes, one in the field of chemistry and one in peace. These were for his work on the structure of proteins and his advocacy for nuclear disarmament.

- Rachel Carson, a marine biologist and conservationist, was credited with starting the modern environmental movement with her book "Silent Spring."

- John Muir was a naturalist and conservationist who played a crucial role in creating the National Park Service.

James Watson and Francis Crick discovered the structure of

- DNA, which revolutionized the field of genetics and led to numerous medical and scientific advancements.

- J. Robert Oppenheimer was once a student of physicist and philosopher Erwin Schrödinger, who was known for his thought experiments involving quantum mechanics.

- Stephen Hawking once lost a bet to physicist Kip Thorne over the existence of black hole event horizons and had to publicly acknowledge that he had lost the bet. He later changed his view again on this concept in 2004 and published a paper arguing that information is lost in black holes.

- Neil Armstrong is known worldwide for being the first person to walk on the Moon, but what most people don't know is that he was also a pilot and an engineer.

- The first American woman to ever travel to space was Sally Ride, and she is still the youngest American astronaut to have gone to space.

- George Washington Carver was once offered a job at a salary of $1 million per year (equivalent to over $20 million today) by Henry Ford, but he declined because he wanted to continue his work at Tuskegee University.

- Albert Einstein was offered to become the President of Israel, but he declined the offer.

- At the age of 21, Stephen Hawking received the news that he had motor neuron disease and was given only a few years to live, but he went on to live for over 50 years and contributed significantly to the fields of physics and cosmology.

- Albert Einstein is known to be one of the most famous scientists in history, but most people don't know that he was also a pacifist and an advocate for civil rights.

Chapter 5

First's in Music

- The first song to be played on the radio was "The Birth of the Blues" by Bessie Smith in 1922.

- The first ever rock and roll record to be recorded was "Rocket 88" by Ike Turner in 1951.

- The first ever Grammy Awards ceremony was held in 1959 and honored the best in music from the previous year.

- The first music video to be played on MTV was "Video Killed the Radio Star" by The Buggles in 1981.

- The first rap single to ever reach the top 40 of the Billboard Hot 100 chart was "Rapper's Delight" by The Sugarhill Gang in 1979.

- The first country music record to be released was "The Little Old Log Cabin in the Lane" by Fiddlin' John Carson in 1923.

- The first rock band to feature a black lead singer was The Paul Butterfield Blues Band, formed in 1963.

- The first music festival that was held in the United States was the Newport Folk Festival in 1959.

- The first hip-hop record to be released was "King Tim III (Personality Jock)" by The Fatback Band in 1979.

- The first blues record to be released was "Crazy Blues" by Mamie Smith in 1920.

- The first music video to reach 1 billion views on YouTube was "Gangnam Style" by Psy in 2012.

- The first jazz record released was "Livery Stable Blues" by the Original Dixieland Jass Band in 1917.

- The first electronic music record to be released was "Electronium" by Raymond Scott in 1950.

- The first punk rock record to be released was "Blank Generation" by Richard Hell and the Voidoids in 1977.

- The first grunge record to be released was "Touch Me I'm Sick" by Mudhoney in 1988.

- The first metal record to be released was "Black Sabbath" by Black Sabbath in 1970.

- The first indie rock record to be released was "The Modern Lovers" by The Modern Lovers in 1976.

- The first hip-hop record to be certified gold was "Rapper's Delight" by The Sugarhill Gang in 1979.

- The first country record to be certified platinum was "Garth Brooks" by Garth Brooks in 1992.

- The first electronic music festival to be held in the United States was the Electric Daisy Carnival in 1997.

Chapter 6

Curious facts about the United States

- The world's largest ball of twine is a roadside attraction located in Cawker City, Kansas. The ball of twine was started by a local farmer named Frank Stoeber in 1953, and over the years, it has grown to an enormous size, weighing over 17,000 pounds (7.7 tonnes) and measuring more than 40 feet (12 meters) in circumference. It is made from over 7 million feet (2133 kilometers/ 1325 miles) of twine, and it has been recognized by the Guinness World Record as the largest ball of twine in the world. It is a popular tourist attraction, and it is a beloved part of the community in Cawker City.

- The United States is the nation with the most people, over 2 million, in prison.

- The U.S. has the largest military budget worldwide, with a budget of over $700 billion in 2021.

- Jousting is considered the official state sport of Maryland. It is a traditional medieval sport involving two riders on horseback, charging each other with lances to knock the other rider off their horse. Jousting was popular in Europe in the Middle Ages and has become popular again in modern times as a form of historical reenactment. In Maryland, jousting is considered an essential part of the state's history and cultural heritage, and it was officially designated as the state sport in 1962. However, despite being the official state sport, jousting is not a widely practiced sport in Maryland, and it is mainly performed as a form of entertainment at historical reenactments and festivals.

- The first Thanksgiving was not a feast between the Pilgrims and the Native Americans but rather a three-day religious celebration held by the Pilgrims in 1621 to give thanks for their safe journey to the New World.

- In 1947, a group of UFO enthusiasts in Roswell, New Mexico claimed that a flying saucer had crashed in the desert nearby. The incident is remembered as the "Roswell UFO incident," and it has sparked numerous conspiracy theories and debates about the existence of extraterrestrial life.

- The tallest mountain in the world is not Mount Everest, but Mauna Kea, a mountain in Hawaii that extends more than 10,000 meters (33,000 feet) from the ocean floor.

- The Declaration of Independence wasn't actually signed by all the founding fathers on July 4th, 1776. Most signed it on August 2nd, and some even signed it later in the year.

- The United States has more billionaires per capita than any other country.

- The United States has more tornadoes per year than any other country worldwide.

- The Grand Canyon, one of the most iconic natural landmarks in the United States, was formed over millions of years by the erosion of the Colorado River.

- Las Vegas, known for its casinos and bright lights, was originally a stopover for travelers on their way to Los Angeles.

- The Liberty Bell, a famous symbol of American independence, was originally cast as a signal bell for the Pennsylvania State House (now commonly known as Independence Hall) in 1752.

- The United States has more gun ownership per capita than any other country.

- The United States has over 200 million registered vehicles, making it the country with the most registered vehicles in the world.

- In 1933, a group of unemployed World War I veterans, known as the Bonus Army, camped out in Washington, D.C., to demand cash payments promised to them in a future bill. President Hoover ordered the Army to remove them, leading to a confrontation that left two veterans dead.

- The United States, the third largest country worldwide by land area, is covering almost 10 million square kilometers.

- The U.S. has a diverse population, with people from several different racial and ethnic backgrounds.

- The U.S. has a federal system of government, with powers divided between the federal government and the states.

- Allegedly, In 1947, a UFO crashed in Roswell, New Mexico, leading to widespread speculation that the government covered up the crash and that the military had recovered alien bodies.

- The U.S. has a presidential system of government, with the president serving as both the head of state and also the head of government.

- The U.S. has a market-based economy, meaning businesses are free to operate and compete with one another.

- The U.S. is home to many famous landmarks, including the Grand Canyon, Yellowstone National Park, and the Statue of Liberty.

- The U.S. has a rich cultural history, with a great variety of traditions and customs.

- In 1996, the FBI's Hostage Rescue Team attempted to end a standoff with the anti-government group known as the Montana Freeman, which resulted in an intense gun battle and the deaths of one federal agent and one Freeman member.

- The U.S. is home to many famous cultural institutions, such as the Metropolitan Museum of Art, the Smithsonian Institution, and the Kennedy Center for the Performing Arts.

- The U.S. has a long history of immigration, with many people coming from all over the world to live and work there.

- The U.S. is home to many world-renowned universities, including Harvard, Yale, and Stanford.

- The U.S. is home to many professional sports leagues, including the NFL, NBA, MLB, and NHL.

- In 2002, an unknown individual, who would become known as the "Beltway Sniper," terrorized the Washington, D.C., area with a series of random shootings, killing 10 people over the course of three weeks.

- The U.S. is home to various climates, ranging from cold and snowy in the north to hot and humid in the south.

- The U.S. is home to many different types of cuisine, including Italian, Chinese, Mexican, and American.

- The U.S. is home to many famous writers and poets, including Edgar Allan Poe, Mark Twain, and Emily Dickinson.

- In 2011, a group of amateur treasure hunters discovered $1.8 million in buried treasure on an island off the coast of Florida. It was later revealed to be from a famous treasure hunter, Forrest Fenn's, treasure hunt that he had put out.

- The U.S. is home to many famous musicians and bands, including Elvis Presley and Madonna.

- The U.S. is home to many famous actors and actresses, including Tom Hanks, Meryl Streep, and Denzel Washington.

- The U.S. is home to many famous artists, including Georgia O'Keeffe, Jackson Pollock, and Frederic Church.

- In 1963, a group of inmates at Alcatraz prison, known as the "Battle of Alcatraz," attempted to escape the island prison but were ultimately unsuccessful. Two guards were killed, and several inmates were killed or injured.

- The U.S. is home to many famous architects, including Frank Lloyd Wright and Louis Sullivan.

- The U.S. is home to many famous inventors, like Thomas Edison and Alexander Graham Bell.

- In 1960, a group of civil rights activists, known as the "Greensboro Four," staged a sit-in at a Woolworth's lunch counter in

Greensboro, North Carolina, to protest the store's policy of racial segregation.

- The U.S. is home to many famous scientists, including Albert Einstein, Benjamin Franklin and Grace Murray Hopper.

- The U.S. is home to many famous business leaders, including Steve Jobs and Bill Gates.

- The United States has the longest coastline in the world, and outside the coast of Texas, you can also find the longest continuous barrier island in the world. This island is known as Padre Island, stretching over 130 miles (209 km). It is home to various wildlife, including sea turtles and migratory birds, and is a popular destination for fishing and other outdoor activities. Additionally, Padre Island is one of the country's few remaining undeveloped barrier islands, making it a unique and valuable ecological resource.

- The U.S. is home to many famous politicians, including George Washington, Abraham Lincoln, and John F. Kennedy.

- The U.S. is home to many famous athletes, including Michael Jordan, LeBron James, and Serena Williams.

- In 1972, a group of thieves stole $2.5 million from a Brink's armored truck in Boston in what would be known as the "Boston Brink's Robbery." It remains one of the largest cash thefts in U.S. history.

- The U.S. is home to many famous landmarks, including Mount Rushmore, the Golden Gate Bridge, and the Hollywood Sign.

- The United States use more oil than any other country in the world.

The United States has more retail shopping malls than any other

- country.

- The United States contains more public libraries than any other country in the world.

- The United States has more law enforcement officers per capita than any other country worldwide.

- The United States has the most fast food restaurants per capita globally.

- The United States is home to the largest known volcano in the world, Mauna Loa, in Hawaii.

- In 1979, the "Jonestown Massacre" occurred in which over 900 members of the Peoples Temple, a cult led by Jim Jones, died of mass murder-suicide, or execution in the jungle of Guyana.

Chapter 7

Curious facts about American sport

- Baseball was the first professional sport played in the United States. The first professional game was played in 1869 between the Cincinnati Red Stockings and the Brooklyn Eagles. The Cincinnati Red Stockings won the game.

- The first ever modern Olympic Games were held in Athens, Greece, in 1896. The United States was one of the 14 countries that participated in the games, and American James B. Connolly won the first gold medal in the modern Olympic Games.

- The first Super Bowl took place in 1967, and the teams competing were the Green Bay Packers and the Kansas City Chiefs. The Green Bay Packers won the game.

- Michael Jordan, one of the most famous basketball players of all time, is also a successful businessman and owns the Charlotte Hornets NBA team.

- The first basketball game took place in December 1891 at a YMCA in Springfield, Massachusetts. The game was invented by Canadian physical education instructor James Naismith.

- The first professional American football game was played in 1895 between the Allegheny Athletic Association and the Pittsburgh Athletic Club. The Allegheny Athletic Association won the game.

- The first U.S. Open golf tournament was held in 1895 at the Newport Golf and Country Club in Rhode Island. Horace Rawlins won, a 21-year-old Englishman.

- The first ever modern World Series was played in 1903 between the Boston Americans and the Pittsburgh Pirates. The Boston Americans won the series.

- The first professional boxing match was held in 1892 between John L. Sullivan and Jack Burke in New Orleans, Louisiana. Sullivan won the fight in the first round.

- The first modern Olympic Winter Games were held in Chamonix, France, in 1924. The United States sent a team of six athletes who competed in the ice hockey and speed skating events.

- The first World Cup soccer tournament was held in 1930 in Uruguay. The United States did not take part in the tournament, but the team has qualified for every World Cup since 1990.

- The first Stanley Cup, the National Hockey League championship trophy (NHL), was awarded in 1893. The Montreal Hockey Club was the winner.

- The first World Series of Poker was held in 1970 at the Binion's Horseshoe Casino in Las Vegas, Nevada. The winner was Johnny Moss, a professional poker player.

- The first Major League Soccer (MLS) season was held in 1996. The league currently has 26 teams, with expansion plans for more teams in the future.

- The first Major League Baseball (MLB) game was played on April 22, 1876, between the Boston Red Stockings and the Philadelphia Athletics.

Chapter 8

Curious facts about space

- The universe is estimated to be around 13.8 billion years old.

- The temperature in space is extremely cold, with an average temperature of about -454.81°F (-270°C).

- The solar system is part of the Milky Way galaxy, containing about 200 billion stars.

- As there is no air in space, astronauts need to wear specialized suits to breathe.

- The International Space Station (ISS) is considered the largest man-made object in space, and it orbits the Earth at an altitude of roughly 250 miles (400 kilometers).

- The Moon is the Earth's only natural satellite, and it is about 238,855 miles (384,400 kilometers) away from the Earth.

- There are over 8,000 known asteroids in our solar system, and many more that have yet to be discovered.

- Our solar system contains 9 planets, and listed in order from the Sun, they are called Mercury, Venus, Earth, Mars, Jupiter, Saturn, Uranus, Neptune, and Pluto.

- There are more than about 100 billion galaxies in the visible universe, each one containing millions or billions of stars.

- The fastest spacecraft ever launched is NASA's Parker Solar Probe, which reached a speed of 430,000 miles per hour (690,000 km/h) in 2021.

- There have been a total of about 536 people who have been to space as of 2021.

- The surface area of the Moon measures about 14.6 million square miles (38 million square kilometers), which is about the same as the land area of Africa.

- The Sun is considered a star, and it is the star closest to Earth, about 93 million miles (150 million kilometers) away.

- The Sun is roughly 4.6 billion years old and is expected to continue burning for another 5 billion years.

- The Milky Way is estimated to be about 13.51 billion years old.

- The Hubble Space Telescope, launched in 1990, has captured some of the most stunning images of the universe, including distant galaxies, nebulae, and star clusters.

- Jupiter is the biggest of the planets in our solar system. It is about 11 times the size of Earth.

- There are three types of galaxies: spiral, elliptical, and irregular. The Milky Way is a barred spiral galaxy.

- The first human landing on the Moon took place on July 20, 1969, when NASA's Apollo 11 mission successfully landed astronauts Neil Armstrong and Edwin "Buzz" Aldrin on the lunar surface.

- The first spacecraft to ever land on another planet was NASA's Viking 1, which landed on Mars in 1976. Since then, several other spacecraft have explored Mars, including the Mars rover Curiosity, which is currently active on the planet's surface.

- The temperature on the surface of Venus, the hottest planet in our solar system, can reach up to 864°F (462°C), which is hot enough to melt lead.

- The largest asteroid in our solar system is Ceres, which is about 590 miles (940 kilometers) in diameter and is classified as a dwarf planet.

- There are over 4,000 known exoplanets or planets outside our solar system, and many more are expected to be discovered in the future.

- The first satellite, Sputnik 1, was launched into orbit by the Soviet Union in 1957.

- The International Space Station is home to astronauts from various countries, including the United States, Russia, Japan, and Canada.

- There are several space agencies around the world, including NASA (United States), Roscosmos (Russia), and the European Space Agency (Europe).

- The first human spaceflight was conducted by the Soviet Union in 1961 when Yuri Gagarin became the first person to orbit the

Earth.

- The Apollo 11 mission, which took the first humans on the Moon, was launched from the Kennedy Space Center in the state of Florida on July 16, 1969.

- The surface of the planet Mars is rocky and dusty, and it has the largest volcano in the solar system, Olympus Mons. It is about 16 miles (26 kilometers) tall and about 370 miles (600 kilometers) wide.

- The Earth is the third planet from the Sun and is the only known planet supporting life.

- The Earth is the fifth densest planet in the solar system, and it is made up of three key layers: the crust, the mantle, and the core.

- Mars is commonly referred to as the "Red Planet" because its surface is covered in iron oxide, or rust, which gives it a reddish appearance.

- Saturn is known for its beautiful rings, which are made up of billions of small ice and rock particles.

- Uranus is the coldest of the planets in the solar system, with an average temperature of about -353°F (-214°C).

- Neptune has the most powerful winds in the solar system, with gusts reaching up to 1,500 mph (2,400 km/h).

- Pluto was classified as a planet until 2006, but was then reclassified as a "dwarf planet."

- The Kuiper Belt is a region beyond Neptune home to many small, icy objects, including Pluto. The Kuiper Belt is thought to contain thousands or even millions of these objects.

- The surface of Mercury is rocky and covered in craters, and it has a very thin atmosphere.

- Venus is the brightest planet and can often be seen from Earth just before sunrise or just after sunset.

- The Earth is the only planet in our solar system that contains liquid water on its surface, which is essential for life as we know it.

- Jupiter's Great Red Spot is an enormous storm that has been blazing for hundreds of years, and it is large enough to fit three Earths side by side.

- Saturn's rings consists of billions of small ice and rock particles that are held in place by the planet's gravity.

- Uranus is tilted on its side, so its north and south poles are located where most other planets have their equators.

- Neptune has a faint ring system that is made up of dust and small particles.

- Pluto is the smallest of the planets in our solar system, and it is about two-thirds the size of Earth's moon.

- The Kuiper Belt is home to many small, icy objects that are thought to be leftovers from the solar system's formation. Some of these objects, known as Kuiper Belt Objects (KBOs), are thought to be the building blocks for larger objects like Pluto.

- Astronauts can get taller while in space because the lack of gravity causes their spines to stretch.

- The astronauts manning the International Space Station (ISS) have to exercise about two hours a day to prevent muscle and bone loss.

- The ISS orbits around the Earth at a speed of about 17,500 mph, which means that astronauts on the ISS experience 16 sunrises and sunsets every 24 hours.

- Astronauts can't cry in space because the lack of gravity causes tears to form balls instead of streaming down their faces.

- The Apollo 11 astronauts, Neil Armstrong and Edwin "Buzz" Aldrin, took a plaque to the Moon that had the inscription, "Here men from the planet Earth first set foot upon the Moon, July 1969 A.D. We came in peace for all mankind".

- On 12 April 1961, Yuri Gagarin, a Soviet citizen, was the first astronaut to go to space.

- In 1961, Alan Shepard was the first American astronaut to go to space and the second person worldwide. In 1971, he also became the fifth and oldest person to walk on the Moon.

- There have been over 500 people from more than 40 countries who have gone to space.

- The Moon is considered the fifth largest natural satellite in the solar system and is about one-quarter the size of Earth.

- The Moon's surface is rocky and dusty, and it has no atmosphere or water.

- The Moon's surface temperature can range from about -280 degrees Fahrenheit at night to about 250 degrees Fahrenheit during the day.

- The Moon has a very thin atmosphere made up of gases like helium, neon, and hydrogen, which are released from the surface by the solar wind.

- The Moon's surface is covered with craters, mountains, and flat plains called "maria," which are thought to be ancient lava flows.

- The Moon has not got any light of its own and reflects light from the Sun, which is why it appears to glow in the sky at night.

- The Moon has a powerful effect on Earth, including controlling the tides and causing the Earth's rotation to slow down over time.

- There have been six manned missions to the Moon, the first of which was the Apollo 11 mission in 1969.

- The Sun is about 109 times wider than Earth and about 330,000 times more massive.

- The Sun is a giant ball of gas mostly containing hydrogen and helium, and it is held together by its own gravity.

- The surface temperature on the Sun is about 10,000 degrees Fahrenheit, and its core temperature is about 27 million degrees Fahrenheit.

- The Sun produces energy through a process called nuclear fusion, in which hydrogen atoms combine to form helium.

- The Sun's energy is responsible for warming the Earth and is also the primary source of light for the solar system.

- The Sun has a powerful magnetic field that produces solar winds, which can affect Earth's atmosphere and climate.

- The Sun is thought to be about 4.6 billion years old and expected to remain stable for another 5 billion years. After that, it is expected to expand and become a giant red star, swallowing up planets like Earth.

- The nearest star to Earth, other than the Sun, is Proxima Centauri, about 4.2 light-years away.

- The Moon's surface is covered in a layer of fine, powdery dust called regolith, which was formed by meteor impacts over billions of years.

- There are over 200 known moons in the solar system.

- The atmosphere on Saturn is made up of mostly hydrogen and helium, and the planet has over 60 moons.

- The surface of Neptune is covered in a layer of frozen methane, which gives the planet its blue color.

- The surface of Uranus is covered in a layer of methane and ammonia ice, which gives the planet its blue-green color.

- The atmosphere on Jupiter is made up of mostly hydrogen and helium, and the planet has over 60 moons.

- The surface of Pluto is covered in a layer of frozen methane, which gives the planet its reddish color.

- There are over 1,000 known asteroids in the asteroid belt between Mars and Jupiter.

- The Sun's surface is about 10,000 degrees Fahrenheit (5,500 degrees Celsius).

- Mars has two small moons, Phobos and Deimos.

- The surface of Venus is covered in a layer of sulfuric acid clouds, which gives the planet its orange-yellow color.

- The surface of Earth is made up of 70% water and 30% land.

- There are over 8,000 known comets in the solar system.

- The surface of Jupiter is made up of mostly gas and has no solid surface.

Chapter 9

Interesting and fun facts about musical instruments

- The oldest known musical instrument is a flute made out of bone, which was discovered in Germany and is believed to be over 35,000 years old.

- The violin is often considered the most challenging instrument to learn to play due to its small size and the intricate techniques required to play it properly.

- The guitar has a rich history and has been played by musicians worldwide for centuries. It has been used in various musical styles, including rock, jazz, and folk music.

- The saxophone was invented by a Belgian musician named Adolphe Sax in the 1840s. It was originally intended to be a hybrid of the woodwind and brass families, but it became a unique instrument in its own right.

- The drums are integral to many musical styles and have been used in various forms for centuries. They are often considered the backbone of a band or ensemble and provide the rhythmic foundation for the music.

- The banjo, a popular bluegrass, and folk music instrument, has African roots. Its origins can be sketched back to the West African instrument called the akonting, which was brought in to the United States by enslaved Africans.

- The piano is a great instrument that can be played in various styles, including classical, jazz, and pop. It is also one of the largest and most complex musical instruments, with over 12,000 parts.

- The ukulele, a small stringed instrument often associated with Hawaiian music, was actually introduced to Hawaii by the Portuguese immigrants in the late 19th century.

- The sitar, a popular instrument in Indian classical music, has a unique sound due to its resonance chamber, which is made from a dried gourd.

- The cello is a beautiful and powerful string instrument played with a bow. It has a rich and varied history and was developed during the late Renaissance period as an evolution of smaller stringed instruments such as the viola da braccio. The cello, short for violoncello, was created to fill the need for a deeper, more resonant bass sound in orchestras and chamber music ensembles.

- The didgeridoo, a traditional Australian instrument, is made from a hollowed-out tree branch and is played by buzzing the lips into the instrument while simultaneously playing a melody with the tongue.

- The clarinet is a woodwind instrument played by blowing into a reed and fingering the keys. During World War 2, it was used in a unique and creative way by French resistance fighters to send coded messages. The resistance would play specific songs on the clarinet, each of which had a different meaning. For example, one piece would signal an upcoming attack, while another would signal a change in meeting location. The Germans were unaware of the coded messages and would not suspect a simple musical performance as a means of communication. This allowed the resistance to communicate secretly and effectively without detection. This technique was so successful that it was also used in other parts of Europe.

- The accordion, a popular instrument in folk music, was invented in Germany in the early 19th century. It is played by pressing buttons or keys to open and close reeds, which produce sound when air is forced through them.

- The trumpet is a brass instrument that has a rich and varied history. It has been used in many different musical styles but has been a staple in jazz music since the genre's early days. One of the most notable jazz trumpet players is Louis Armstrong, considered one of the most influential figures in jazz history. Armstrong's innovative playing style and virtuosic technique revolutionized the way the trumpet was played in jazz music.

- The maracas, a popular percussion instrument often associated with Latin American music, were originally used by indigenous peoples in South America as a form of communication.

- The harp is a beautiful and intricate instrument that uses fingers to pluck the strings. The pedal harp, commonly known as the concert harp, was developed in the early 19th century by a French instrument maker named Sébastien Érard. It is considered the most advanced and versatile type of harp and is distinctive for its use of pedals that change the pitch of the strings, allowing for a broader range of notes and greater expression. This was a significant improvement over previous harps, which required the harpist to manually change the pitch of the strings. This made the harp much more versatile and expressive and quickly became the standard for professional harpists.

- The koto, a traditional Japanese string instrument, has a distinctive sound due to its 13 strings, which are made of silk and are stretched over a wooden soundboard. It has been a part of Japanese culture for centuries, and it has traditionally been associated with classical music and court music. However, in the 20th century, a group of musicians known as the "New Wave" began experimenting with the koto, incorporating it into new and innovative styles of music, such as jazz and rock. One of the most notable figures of this movement is a koto player and composer named Michio Miyagi. Miyagi was a pioneer in using the koto in contemporary music and is credited with creating a new style of koto music that blended traditional and modern elements. The New Wave movement and musicians like Miyagi helped to bring the koto to a new audience and helped to revitalize interest in the instrument. Today, the koto is still an important part of traditional Japanese music, but it has also found a new place in contemporary music and is played by musicians worldwide.

- The xylophone, a popular percussion instrument, is made of wooden bars that are struck with small hammers to produce sound. The thickness of the bars determines the pitch of the sound. It is likely to have originated in Africa and was made from local materials such as bamboo or hardwood. It was then brought to Asia by traders and other travelers and quickly adopted by the local cultures. It was particularly popular in Indonesia and the Philippines and became a central part of traditional music. From there, it was brought to Europe by colonizers and traders, where it was further developed and eventually became a part of Western classical music.

- The oud, a popular instrument in Middle Eastern and North African music, has a distinctive sound due to its pear-shaped body and 11 strings tuned in a unique pattern. It has likely originated in ancient Mesopotamia and has been played for thousands of years.

- The guzheng, commonly known as the Chinese zither, is a traditional Chinese musical instrument with a history dating back over 2,500 years. The instrument has a long, narrow rectangular shape with strings stretched over a wooden frame. People play it by plucking the strings with plectra attached to the fingers. Also, the guzheng is not just a musical instrument but also a cultural symbol representing Chinese traditional culture and its history. As a result, it's often featured in traditional Chinese performances.

Chapter 10

Interesting facts about American states

- Alabama is home to the oldest city in the United States, Mobile, founded by French colonists in 1702.

- Alaska is the largest state in the United States, covering an area of 663,267 square miles (1,717,854 square kilometers). It is over twice the size of Texas, the second-largest state.

- Arizona is home to the Grand Canyon, and it is one of the most iconic natural landmarks in the United States. The Grand Canyon is roughly 277 miles (446 kilometers) long, up to about 18 miles (29 kilometers) wide, and over a mile deep.

- Arkansas is home to Hot Springs National Park, the oldest of the national parks in the United States. It was established in 1832.

- California is home to Hollywood, the entertainment capital of the world. It is also home to Silicon Valley, the hub of the tech industry.

- Colorado is home to the Rocky Mountain National Park, which is home to over 300 miles (483 kilometers) of hiking trails and more than 60 peaks that are over 12,000 feet (3657 meters) tall.

- Connecticut is home to Yale University, founded in 1701, and one of the oldest universities in the United States.

- Delaware is the second-smallest of the state in the United States, covering an area of just 1,955 square miles (5063 square kilometers). It is also the only state that does not have any national parks.

- Florida is home to Everglades National Park, the largest subtropical wilderness in the United States. The park is home to over 350 species of birds and more than 50 species of reptiles.

- Georgia is home to the largest public urban park in the United States, the Piedmont Park in Atlanta. The park covers over 185 acres (0.75 square kilometers or 0.29 square miles) and is a popular spot for outdoor concerts and events.

- Hawaii is the only U.S. state entirely made up of islands. It is also the only state that grows coffee.

- Idaho is home to the Snake River, the largest tributary of the Columbia River. The Snake River is about 1,078 miles (1735 kilometers) long and flows through three states: Wyoming, Idaho, and Washington.

- Illinois is home to the Willis Tower (formerly known as the Sears Tower), the tallest building in the world when completed in 1974. It is currently the second-tallest building in the United States.

- Indiana is home to the Indianapolis 500, a 500-mile (805 kilometers) race held annually at the Indianapolis Motor Speedway. It is amongst the most prestigious races globally and often referred to as the "Greatest Spectacle in Racing."

Iowa is home to the Field of Dreams, a baseball diamond built in

- the middle of a cornfield in Dyersville, Iowa. The field was made famous by the 1989 movie "Field of Dreams," which was filmed on location.

- Kansas is home to the Tallgrass Prairie National Preserve, which is the largest protected area of tallgrass prairie in the United States. The preserve is home to over 500 species of plants and animals.

- Kentucky is home to the Kentucky Derby, a horse race held yearly at Churchill Downs in Louisville. The Kentucky Derby is the oldest regularly held sporting event in the United States.

- Louisiana is home to the New Orleans Jazz & Heritage Festival, which is one of the largest music festivals in the United States. The festival features a wide variety of musical styles, including jazz, blues, rock, and hip-hop.

Chapter 11

Curious facts about American geography

- The United States has over 3,000 counties, which are the primary administrative divisions in the country.

- The United States has 50 states plus the District of Columbia, which is the capital of the United States.

- The United States is the fourth biggest country worldwide by land area, covering over 3.8 million square miles (9.8 million square kilometers).

- The United States has diverse landscapes and climates, ranging from tropical rainforests in Hawaii to arid deserts in the Southwest.

- The United States has over 250,000 rivers, including the Mississippi River, the second-longest river in North America.

- The United States has over 100,000 lakes, including the Great Lakes, a group of five large freshwater lakes located on the border between the United States and Canada.

- The United States has over 50 mountain ranges, including the Rocky Mountains, the highest mountain range in North America.

- The United States has over 3,000 national parks, which are protected areas managed by the National Park Service. These parks include some of the most iconic natural landmarks in the country, such as Yellowstone National Park and Yosemite National Park.

- The United States has over 50,000 miles (80,467 kilometers) of coastline, including the Gulf Coast, the Atlantic Coast, and the Pacific Coast.

- The United States has over 3,000 islands, including the Hawaiian Islands, located in the Pacific Ocean.

- The United States is home to a wide variety of wildlife, including over 1,500 species of birds and over 400 species of mammals. It is also home to many unique plant species, including cacti, palm, and redwood.

- The U.S. is home to a number of iconic landmarks, including the Statue of Liberty, the Grand Canyon, the Golden Gate Bridge, and many others.

Chapter 12

Interesting facts and stories about American culture

- America is home to a wide variety of bizarre and unusual roadside attractions, such as the World's Largest Ball of Twine, the World's Largest Catsup Bottle, and the World's Largest Peanut.

- "The Melting Pot" is a term used to describe the diverse range of cultures in the United States, with influences from various countries and traditions. Big cities such as New York City, Los Angeles, and San Francisco are known for their vibrant ethnic neighborhoods, such as Little Italy, Chinatown, and Little Havana. These have become famous tourist destinations and are a testament to the cultural diversity of the United States. Despite the challenges, America's cultural diversity is one of its greatest strengths. It has led to a rich tapestry of customs, traditions, and cuisines that make the country unique. The blending of cultures has also led to new, hybrid forms of art, music, and cuisine that are uniquely American.

- The United States is known for its fast food culture. In the 1950s, many fast food chains, such as McDonald's, Burger King, and KFC, began to expand rapidly across the country, revolutionizing the restaurant industry and changing how Americans ate. Fast food has also become a cultural export, and American fast food chains can be found worldwide, from Europe to Asia to Africa. Recently, many fast-food chains have started to offer more nutritious menu items, and there has been a growing focus on healthier menu options and an interest in farm-to-table and organic food.

- Elvis Presley, the "King of Rock and Roll," was also an avid collector of police badges and owned over 100 of them.

- The art of yard gnome hunting, also known as gnoming, is a light-hearted and playful activity that involves stealing or "kidnapping" small lawn ornaments known as yard gnomes and then placing them in different locations as a form of pranks or jokes. Yard gnome hunting is often done by groups of friends or teenagers as a way to have fun and pass the time, and it has become a popular activity in some communities. While yard gnome hunting is generally considered to be harmless and good-natured, it is important to remember that it is still a form of trespassing and property damage, and it is important to seek permission before moving or taking someone else's property.

- The United States has a strong coffee culture, with various coffee shops and chains, such as Starbucks and other specialty coffee shops. In the early 1980s, a group of coffee enthusiasts began experimenting with new brewing methods and exploring the nuances of different beans and roasts. This led to a new type of coffee culture emphasizing quality over convenience, celebrating the art and science of coffee, and characterized by small, independent coffee shops that offered various beans and brewing methods. It also featured baristas trained to brew coffee to perfection and create latte art. This specialty coffee culture spread quickly, and by the late 1990s, specialty coffee shops could be found in cities across the country.

- The U.S. has a rich musical history, with a variety of genres, including jazz, blues, rock and roll, and hip hop, all having originated in the country.

- Marilyn Monroe, one of the most iconic actresses of all time, was a talented singer and model before becoming an actress.

- In the 1970s, the United States government conducted a secret operation known as "Project MKUltra," using drugs, hypnosis, and other methods to control people's minds.

- The tradition of Groundhog Day is based on a combination of ancient European weather lore and the traditions of Native American groups who lived in the area that is now the United States. The holiday has its roots in the practices of the Punxsutawney Groundhog Club, a group of hunters and naturalists who began observing and predicting the weather based on the behavior of groundhogs in the late 1800s. The holiday gained widespread popularity in the United States in the 20th century, thanks in part to the widespread coverage of the annual Groundhog Day event in Punxsutawney, Pennsylvania. Today, Groundhog Day is celebrated in many parts of the United States and Canada, and it has become a popular holiday enjoyed by people of all ages.

- The United States is home to many iconic movies and TV shows, such as "Star Wars," "The Sopranos," and "Friends."

- Oprah Winfrey, one of the most influential women in media, was the first black woman to own and host a nationally syndicated television show.

- The United States has a strong sports culture, with various popular sports, such as football, basketball, and baseball.

- Many cultural and historical landmarks are scattered throughout The United States, including the Independence Hall in Philadelphia, the Lincoln Memorial in Washington D.C., and the Statue of Liberty in New York City.

- The United States has a strong consumer culture, with many people focused on buying and owning material possessions. From the early 20th century, American companies began to use advertising and consumerism to drive economic growth and shape culture. As a result, advertisements and consumerism have played a significant role in shaping American culture, creating a desire for new products, and shaping ideals and desires.

- In the 1960s, the American counterculture movement, characterized by the use of drugs, rejection of mainstream values, and experiments with alternative lifestyles, had a significant impact on the country's politics and social norms.

- Americans love pets, with many people owning dogs, cats, and other animals as companions.

- America is home to many competitive eating contests, such as the Nathan's Hot Dog Eating Contest on July 4th and the World Lobster Eating Championship.

- The first Thanksgiving celebration in America was held in 1621 by the Pilgrims, who had settled in Plymouth, Massachusetts. However, this celebration was not an annual event and did not become a national holiday until the 19th century.

- America's love for coffee has created jobs and business opportunities for millions of people, from farmers in developing countries to baristas and entrepreneurs in the United States. In addition, the coffee shop has become an essential social space where people can meet to catch up, work, or relax. There has been an increased interest in sustainability in the coffee industry in recent years, with more and more coffee shops sourcing beans from fair trade and organic farms. Also, more and more people are interested in the origins of the beans they consume. Today, the American coffee culture is more diverse and dynamic than ever, with a wide range of options available to coffee lovers, from traditional drip coffee to the latest specialty coffee trends.

- The United States has a strong fast-fashion culture, with many Americans frequently buying and disposing of cheap clothing.

- In the 1920s, a group of wealthy young Americans known as the "Roaring Twenties Flappers" gained notoriety for their unconventional lifestyle, which included bobbing their hair, wearing short skirts, and dancing provocatively.

- The United States has a strong work culture, with many people working long hours and placing a high value on career success.

- In the 1990s, a group of people known as the "Wenatchee sex ring" were falsely accused of engaging in satanic ritual abuse and child sexual abuse based on coerced and faulty testimony.

- Americans are known for their love of cars, with many people owning and driving their own vehicles.

- The United States is home to a variety of different cuisines, with influences from a range of different countries, including Italy, China, and Mexico.

- The first shopping mall, Southdale Center, opened in Edina, Minnesota, in 1956, and it was an immediate success. The mall featured a wide variety of stores, a food court, and even a small amusement park, all under one roof. Shopping malls quickly spread across the country, becoming a staple of American consumer culture. They became popular hangout places for teenagers and families and a destination for shopping, entertainment, and socializing.

- In the 1980s, a series of murders known as the "Satanic Panic" led many people in the United States to believe that there was a widespread conspiracy of Satanists committing ritual abuse and murder. It is now widely recognized that the "Satanic Panic" was a moral panic fueled by misinformation and irrational fears rather than any actual evidence of widespread satanic cults.

- The United States has a strong technology culture, with many people using smartphones, tablets, and other devices daily.

- Halloween is popular in America, with many people participating in Halloween traditions, such as dressing up in costumes and trick-or-treating.

- Lady Gaga, one of the most successful pop stars of all time, is also an actress and has won a Golden Globe award for her role in the TV show "American Horror Story."

- The United States has a strong gun culture, with many owning guns for self-defense and recreational purposes.

- The United States is known for its love of sports, with many people following and participating in various sports.

- Cultural holidays are important to Americans, with many people celebrating holidays such as Christmas, Thanksgiving, and Easter.

- In the late 19th and early 20th centuries, it was common for people in the United States to attend "spectacle" events such as live elephant hangings, public executions, and freak shows featuring people with physical abnormalities.

- During the Great Depression, some people in the United States turned to cannibalism due to extreme poverty and food shortages.

- America has a long history of conspiracy theories, ranging from the belief that the government is hiding the truth about aliens to the idea that the moon landing was faked.

- America is home to a large number of theme parks, ranging from small local attractions to massive, world-renowned parks like Disney World and Universal Studios.

- In the early 21st century, the United States saw a rise in "fake news," or misinformation presented as factual news, leading to significant polarization and mistrust in media.

- In the 1970s and 1980s, a number of American chefs began to experiment with combining different ethnic flavors and ingredients to create a new type of cuisine. One of the most famous examples of fusion cuisine is Californian cuisine, which combines elements of French, Italian, and Asian cuisine to create a new and unique style of cooking. Chefs such as Wolfgang Puck, who introduced fusion cuisine to America through his restaurant Spago, were instrumental in popularizing this new style of cooking.

- The United States has over 300 million people, making it the third-most populous country in the world.

- The United States has a diverse range of languages, with English being the most commonly spoken language. However, many other languages are spoken in the United States, including Spanish, Chinese, French, and German.

- In the 1950s, the United States government conducted secret experiments on its own citizens, exposing them to diseases such as syphilis without their knowledge or consent.

- Immigrants from all over the world have brought their own culinary traditions to America, and these have had a profound impact on American cuisine. For example, Chinese immigrants introduced Chinese cuisine to America, while Italian immigrants introduced pizza and pasta, and Mexican immigrants introduced Mexican cuisine. Today, American cuisine is a melting pot of flavors, styles, and traditions, reflecting the diverse backgrounds and experiences of the American people.

- Americans love outdoor recreation, with many people participating in activities such as hiking, camping, and fishing.

- The United States is a federal republic with a government system divided into three branches: the legislative, executive, and judicial branches.

- The United States has a strong economy, with a gross domestic product (GDP) of over $21 trillion. It is one of the largest economies in the world and is home to many of the world's largest companies.

- The United States is a major player in international relations and has a powerful military, with bases and personnel stationed worldwide.

- The United States is a leader in scientific and technological innovation, with many of the world's leading universities and research institutions located within its borders.

Chapter 13

Interesting facts about The American Civil War

- The American Civil War went on from 1861 to 1865 and was one of the deadliest conflicts in American history, with an estimated 750,000 soldiers and civilians losing their lives.

- The key cause of the Civil War was a disagreement between the Northern and Southern states over the issue of slavery. The Southern states wanted to maintain slavery, while the Northern states wanted to end it.

- The Union (also known as the North) was led by President Abraham Lincoln and included 23 states, while the Confederacy (also known as the South) was led by President Jefferson Davis and included 11 states.

- The Union had a larger population and a more industrialized economy, which gave it an advantage in the war. However, the Confederacy had a stronger military tradition and many skilled generals, which helped it to hold its own against the Union for much of the war.

- The Civil War saw the introduction of many new technologies, such as ironclad ships, rifled muskets, and telegraphs used by both sides in the conflict.

- The Civil War was characterized by brutal warfare, with many soldiers dying from disease, starvation, and exposure as well as from combat injuries.

- The Civil War saw the first use of submarines in warfare, with the Union using the USS Alligator and the Confederacy using the CSS Hunley.

- The Civil War was also marked by several significant battles, including the Battle of Bull Run, the Battle of Gettysburg, and the Battle of Antietam.

- The Civil War had a significant impact on the United States, resulting in the abolition of slavery being one of the most important outcomes of the conflict. The Civil War also significantly changed the United States political and social landscape.

- The Civil War is remembered and celebrated in several different ways in the United States, with many Americans visiting Civil War battlefields, museums, and other historical sites to learn about this important period in American history.

Chapter 14

Interesting facts about American History

- In 1864, during the Civil War, Union General William Tecumseh Sherman sent a telegram to President Lincoln saying, "I beg to present you as a Christmas gift, the city of Savannah." He had just captured the city from the Confederacy and wanted to give it to the President as a present.

- The first English settlement in America was not established for the purpose of religious freedom, but rather for economic reasons. The Virginia Company hoped to find gold and other valuable resources in the New World.

- In 1876, a group of cowboys in Texas formed the "Dead Man's Association," which required members to pay a fee and name someone else as their beneficiary. If the member died, the beneficiary would receive the fee. This was essentially an early form of life insurance.

- The Vikings established a settlement in present-day Newfoundland, Canada, around the year 1000, but it was abandoned after a few years due to a lack of resources.

- In 1917, the U.S. government passed the Espionage Act, which made it illegal to interfere with military operations or to promote insubordination in the military. This law was used to arrest and imprison people for expressing anti-war views during World War I. One of the most famous people to be arrested under this law was socialist leader Eugene Debs, who was sentenced to 10 years in prison for giving an anti-war speech.

- In 1939, a man named John D. MacArthur owned a string of laundromats in Chicago and struggled to make ends meet. He decided to try his hand at the insurance business and founded the company that would eventually become known as "Geico." Today, Geico is one of the largest insurance companies in the world.

- In 1969, some Native American activists occupied Alcatraz Island in San Francisco Bay, claiming it as Indian land. They stayed on the island for more than a year, drawing attention to the injustices faced by Native Americans and inspiring a movement for Native American civil rights.

- In 1911, a group of suffragists led by Alice Paul staged a series of protests in Washington, D.C., calling for the right to vote for women. These protests, known as the "Silent Sentinels," involved the women standing quietly with signs outside the White House. As a result, they were often harassed and arrested, and many went on hunger strikes while in jail. The protests eventually helped to secure the passage of the 19th Amendment to the Constitution, which granted women the right to vote.

- In 1962, a man named Walter Cronkite reported on the first live television transmission of manned spaceflight, in which astronaut John Glenn orbited the Earth. Cronkite's excited and emotional reporting on the event earned him the nickname "the most trusted man in America."

- The first settlers in America faced many challenges, including conflict with Native American tribes, disease, and harsh weather conditions. Many of the early settlements were not successful and did not survive.

- In 1980, a group of employees at the Chiat/Day advertising agency in Los Angeles came up with a revolutionary idea for an advertising campaign for a new product called the Apple Macintosh computer. The campaign featured a commercial called "1984," which aired during the Super Bowl and featured a woman running through a dystopian landscape, throwing a hammer at a large screen showing an authoritarian figure. The commercial was a huge success and is now considered one of the most iconic advertisements in history.

- In 1871, a group of African American men in South Carolina formed a secret society called the Knights of Labor. The group was dedicated to fighting for the rights of working people and pushing for social and political change. The Knights of Labor eventually became one of the largest and most influential labor organizations in the country.

- In 1909, a group of African American intellectuals and activists met in New York City to discuss the issues facing their community. This meeting, known as the "Niagara Movement," was led by W.E.B. Du Bois and included such notable figures as Ida B. Wells and William Monroe Trotter. The Niagara Movement was an important precursor to the civil rights movement that took place in the 20th century.

- In 1932, Lindbergh became the first person to fly solo across the Atlantic Ocean. His flight, which took place in a small plane called the "Spirit of St. Louis," was a significant achievement and made him an international celebrity.

- In 1954, a group of African American students in Topeka, Kansas, challenged segregation in public schools by refusing to attend "separate but equal" schools. Their case, known as Brown v. Board of Education, eventually made its way to the U.S. Supreme Court, which ruled segregation in public schools unconstitutional.

- In 1971, a group of activists led by John Kerry (who later became a U.S. Senator and Secretary of State) formed the Vietnam Veterans Against the War group. The group was dedicated to protesting the Vietnam War and advocating for veterans' rights. They were known for their high-profile demonstrations, and their efforts helped to build support for the anti-war movement.

- During the American Revolutionary War, Benjamin Franklin helped design the first American flag with 13 stars and 13 stripes to represent the 13 colonies that declared independence from Great Britain.

- In 1976, a rumor began circulating that a group of terrorists was planning to poison the nation's water supply by putting cyanide in the soap dispensers in public restrooms. The rumor caused widespread panic and led to the removal of soap dispensers from many public restrooms.

- The first successful powered flight in history was made by the Wright brothers in 1903, at Kitty Hawk, North Carolina.

- The first American President to be assassinated was Abraham Lincoln. Abraham was shot at Ford's Theatre in Washington D. C., by the Confederate sympathizer John Wilkes Booth on April 14, 1865.

- The first successful transatlantic telegraph cable that was completed allowed communication between North America and Europe by telegraph for the first time in 1866.

- The U.S. Social Security program was enacted in 1935, during the Great Depression, to provide financial assistance to older Americans and others in need.

- The United States has 50 states, with Alaska being the largest and Hawaii becoming the 50th state in 1959, the most recent addition to the Union.

- The U.S. has a long history of space exploration, with the first manned mission to the moon being the Apollo 11 mission in 1969.

- The U.S. Constitution, signed in 1787, is the oldest and also the shortest written constitution of any major government worldwide.

- In 1871, the Great Chicago Fire was a devastating fire that burned for three days and destroyed a large portion of the city, including many homes and businesses. It is said to have started when a cow knocked over a lantern in a barn.

- The U.S. has a diverse population, with people from many different ethnicities and cultures. In addition, the United States has the largest immigrant population in the world, with more than 44 million immigrants living in the country.

- The first settlers in America were not the first to cultivate tobacco. The native peoples of the Americas had been growing and using tobacco for centuries before the arrival of Europeans.

- The first English settlement in America was not established by a group of families seeking a new life but rather by a group of single men who hoped to find wealth and opportunity in the New World.

- The first known human habitation in the Americas is believed to have occurred during the last ice age when humans migrated across the Bering Strait land bridge between Siberia and Alaska.

- The Declaration of Independence, adopted on July 4, 1776, declared that the 13 colonies were independent of British rule and established the United States as a new nation.

- The first public school in the U.S. was established in Boston in 1635.

- The American Civil War took place from 1861 to 1865, and was a conflict between the Union (the North) and the Confederacy (the South) over issues including slavery and states' rights.

- The U.S. has a strong military, with the U.S. Army, U.S. Navy, U.S. Air Force, and U.S. Marine Corps being the four branches of the military.

- The U.S. has an extensive history of scientific and technological innovation, with many important inventions and discoveries having been made in the country.

- The Great Molasses Flood of 1919 was a sticky, sweet disaster that occurred in Boston, Massachusetts. On a cold January day, a giant tank containing 2.3 million gallons of molasses burst, sending a massive wave of gooey, brown liquid rushing through the streets of the North End neighborhood. The molasses flood moved at 35 mph, knocking over buildings, destroying infrastructure, and causing 21 deaths and 150 injuries. It was a disaster that was both deadly and delicious, as the sticky molasses stuck to everything it touched, making it difficult to clean up and causing a lingering smell of molasses. The Great Molasses Flood is a strange and unforgettable event in the history of Boston and the United States, and it's definitely something you won't find in your average history book!

- In 1835, The New York Sun published a series of articles claiming that a group of astronomers had discovered a civilization of winged humans living on the moon. The articles were widely believed to be true at the time and caused a sensation. It was later revealed that the articles were a hoax, but the story has become a classic example of fake news.

- In 1987, a rumor began circulating that the government was planning to change the design of the American flag. The rumor caused a backlash, and many people started flying the flag as a form of protest.

- The first settlers in America were not English. The first known human habitation in the Americas was by the Clovis culture, which arrived in what is now the southwestern United States around 13,000 years ago. The Clovis culture, named after the city in New Mexico where their distinctive stone tools were first discovered, is the oldest known human culture in the Americas.

- The first European settlers in America were the Vikings, who established a settlement in present-day Newfoundland, Canada, around the year 1000.

- The first English settlement in America was established by the Virginia Company in 1607 at Jamestown, Virginia. The settlers struggled to survive due to a lack of food and supplies, and many died from disease and starvation.

- There is a long tradition of sporting events in the U.S., with some of the most popular sports being American football, basketball, baseball, and ice hockey.

- In 1842, a group of people in New York City declared war on the city's squirrel population, believing that the squirrels were responsible for a series of accidents and mishaps. The "war" resulted in hundreds of squirrels' deaths and several people's arrests.

- The Pilgrims, who established the Plymouth Colony in Massachusetts in 1620, were seeking religious freedom and sought to establish a "City upon a Hill" as a beacon of Protestantism.

- The first enslaved Africans were taken to America in 1619 and were owned by the Virginia Company. Slavery was not legally recognized in the English colonies until 1660 when it was codified in the Virginia code.

- The first Thanksgiving celebration in America was held in 1621 by the Pilgrims, who invited the local Wampanoag tribe to join them in a three-day feast to give thanks for their first successful harvest.

- The first English settlement in America was not established as a democracy. The Virginia Company was a joint-stock corporation that was granted a charter by the English crown to establish a settlement in the New World.

Chapter 15

Fun facts about the history of film

- The first feature-length movie, "The Story of the Kelly Gang," was released in 1906 in Australia. It was followed by the release of "The Great Train Robbery" in the America in 1903, considered the first American feature film.

- During the early years of cinema, many movie theaters were located in amusement parks and were called "nickelodeons" because they charged a nickel for admission.

- The first movie to use synchronized sound was "The Jazz Singer," released in 1927 and starred Al Jolson.

- In the 1930s, the Hays Code, a set of guidelines governing the production of movies, was introduced in the United States, leading to the production of more "moral" films.

- The first movie to be shown on television was "The Wizard of Oz," which aired on CBS in 1956.

- In the 1960s, the "rating system" was introduced in the United States to classify movies based on their content, including G (general audiences), PG (parental guidance suggested), R (restricted), and X (no one under 17 admitted).

- In the 1970s, the home video market exploded with the introduction of the VHS tape, leading to the proliferation of rental stores and the decline of movie theaters.

- In the 1980s, the advent of the CD-ROM and the DVD led to the development of interactive movies, allowing viewers to make choices that affected the film's outcome.

- The first ever feature-length animated movie, "Snow White and the Seven Dwarfs," was released by Disney in 1937.

- In the 1990s, the rise of independent film and the development of computer-generated imagery (CGI) led to the production of more diverse and experimental movies.

Chapter 16

Crimes gone wrong

- The tale of the man who tried to steal the Liberty Bell is a true story that took place in the mid-20th century. In 2003, a man named John Charles Brooke attempted to steal the Liberty Bell, a famous symbol of American independence, from its home in Philadelphia's Independence Hall. Brooke, who was apparently motivated by a desire to sell the bell and make a profit, used a wheelbarrow to try to wheel the bell out of the building. However, authorities quickly caught and arrested him, and the Liberty Bell was returned to its rightful place. Brooke was later sentenced to probation and a fine for his attempted theft. The story of the man who tried to steal the Liberty Bell is a strange and memorable event in American history. It reminds us of the importance of protecting our nation's historical treasures.

- In 2016, a man in California was caught trying to break into a jail. The man was found attempting to climb over the jail's fence and was arrested and charged with an attempted jailbreak.

- In 2018, a man in Ohio was caught trying to steal a police car. The man was found inside the unlocked vehicle, attempting to start it, and was arrested and charged with grand theft auto.

- In 1997, two men attempted to rob a McDonald's restaurant in

New South Wales, Australia. However, they were foiled when they couldn't figure out how to open the cash register and fled the scene empty-handed.

- In 2010, a man in Florida attempted to rob a store while wearing a plastic bag over his head. However, the bag kept slipping down, covering his face and obstructing his vision, making it difficult for him to see and move. He ended up tripping and falling and was arrested by the police.

- In 2016, a man in Ohio attempted to rob a bank but forgot to bring a weapon. He handed the teller a note demanding money and threatening to use a gun, but when the teller asked to see the weapon, the man admitted that he didn't have one and fled the scene.

- In 2019, a man in Virginia was caught trying to steal a helicopter. The man was found inside the helicopter, attempting to start it, and was arrested and charged with grand theft and attempted theft of an aircraft.

- In 2018, a man in Oregon attempted to rob a convenience store but was thwarted when the clerk refused to give him any money and offered him a banana instead. The man fled the scene empty-handed.

- In 2019, a man in England attempted to rob a convenience store by threatening the clerk with a toy gun. However, the clerk recognized the gun as a fake and chased the man out of the store. The man was later arrested by the police.

Chapter 17

Interesting Facts about Native American History

- Native American cultures have a rich tradition of oral story-telling, and many Native American stories have been passed down through generations.

- The Native American concept of time was often different from that of European cultures, with some tribes viewing time as cyclical rather than linear.

- In the mid-20th century, a Native American activist named Vine Deloria Jr. wrote several influential books on Native American issues, including "Custer Died for Your Sins," which helped to bring attention to the struggles of Native American communities.

- Native American cultures often had complex systems of governance, with some tribes having sophisticated systems of leadership and decision-making.

- In the late 19th century, a Native American leader named Geronimo led a series of successful raids against Mexican and American military forces, earning him a reputation as a formidable warrior.

- Native American societies strongly emphasized community and cooperation, and many tribes had systems in place to help ensure that resources were shared fairly.

- Native American cultures had a deep respect for the natural world, and many tribes had spiritual beliefs and practices that were closely connected to the land and its animals.

- Native American medicine and healing practices were highly advanced, and many tribes had their own unique systems of health care.

- In the early 20th century, a Native American man named Charles Eastman (also known as Ohiyesa) became a prominent author and activist, working to improve conditions for Native Americans and promote understanding between Native American and non-Native American cultures.

- Native American cultures have a long history of artistic expression, and many Native American artists are known for their beautiful and intricate works of art.

- Native American cultures have a rich tradition of music and dance, with many tribes having their own unique musical styles and dance forms.

- Native American cultures often had complex systems of trade, and many tribes were skilled traders who exchanged goods and resources with other tribes and with European settlers.

- Some Native American cultures had complex communication systems, including smoke signals and other forms of visual communication.

- Native American cultures had a long history of using natural resources sustainably, and many tribes had systems in place to manage and conserve resources.

- Native American cultures had a rich tradition of spiritual practices and beliefs, including using sacred plants such as tobacco and peyote in traditional ceremonies.

- Native American cultures had a deep understanding of the natural world, and many tribes had their own unique systems of environmental knowledge.

- In the late 19th century, a Native American woman named Sarah Winnemucca fought for the rights of Native Americans and worked to improve conditions for Native American prisoners.

- Native American cultures have a long history of conflict and warfare, with many tribes fighting for control of territory and resources.

- In the early 20th century, a Native American man named Zitkala-Sa (also known as Gertrude Bonnin) fought for the rights of Native Americans and helped to establish the National Council of American Indians.

- Native American cultures have a long history of resistance and activism, and many Native American leaders have fought for the rights and dignity of their communities.

- Native American cultures had a wide variety of traditional clothing, with each tribe having its own unique styles and designs.

- Native American cultures had highly developed systems of agriculture, with many tribes cultivating various crops such as corn, beans, and squash.

- A powwow is a gathering of Indigenous peoples from North America for the purpose of dancing, singing, and socializing. The event is organized by a tribal or inter-tribal council and can feature a variety of dance styles, such as the round dance, the fancy dance, and the traditional dance. Powwows are a way for Indigenous people to come together, celebrate their culture, and pass on their traditions to the next generation.

Chapter 18

Crazy True Stories about Animals

- The elephant is the only mammal that can not jump.

- The blue whale is larger than any animal on Earth, and the adults can reaching lengths of up to 100 feet (30 meters) and weighing as much as 200 tons.

- The octopus is highly intelligent and can use its tentacles to manipulate objects, open jars, and even escape from tanks.

- The hummingbird is the only bird which can fly backward due to the unique structure of its wings.

- The giraffe is taller than any animal in the world, with adults reaching heights of up to 18 feet (5,5 meters).

- The kangaroo can hop at speeds of up to 45 mph (72 km/h) and jump distances of up to 30 feet (9,1 meters).

- The flamingo can filter small crustaceans and algae from the water using its beak, which is specially adapted for this purpose.

- In 2017, a pet cat in England saved its owner's life by waking him up and alerting him to a house fire. The cat, named Smokey, was hailed as a hero and received a medal from the local fire department.

- In 2015, a group of monkeys in Japan were observed using "money" to purchase food and other items from vending machines. The monkeys used tokens they had obtained by exchanging rocks and other objects with researchers.

- In 2016, a group of chimpanzees in Senegal were observed using sticks as tools to fish for termites, a behavior that had previously only been observed in humans.

- In 2017, a cat in the United Kingdom was diagnosed with cancer and it was given only a few months to live. However, the cat, named Oscar, made a full recovery and went on to live for several more years.

- In 2020, a pet dog in the United States saved its owner's life by barking and alerting neighbors to a gas leak in the house. The dog, named Max, was hailed as a hero and received a medal from the local fire department.

- The axolotl, a type of salamander, can regenerate lost limbs and spinal cord tissue.

- The chameleon can change its skin color to blend in with its surroundings. It does this by controlling the pigments in its skin cells and by manipulating tiny muscles that reflect light differently.

- The octopus is a very intelligent and adaptable animal. It can learn through experience, solve problems, and exhibit individual personality traits.

- The pufferfish, also known as a blowfish, can inflate itself to several times its regular size when threatened. It does this by swallowing air or water and filling up a special organ in its body.

- The firefly is capable of producing light through a chemical reaction called bioluminescence. The light is produced in a special organ in the firefly's abdomen and is used to attract mates or prey.

- The African elephant is larger than any other land animal on Earth. It can weigh up to 24,000 pounds (10,886 kilograms) and can live for up to 70 years.

- The giant panda is native to China and is known for its distinctive black-and-white coloring. It feeds almost exclusively on bamboo, which makes up 99% of its diet.

- The Komodo dragon is a monitor lizard native to the Indonesian islands of Komodo, Rinca, and Flores. It is the largest living lizard species and can grow up to 10 feet (3 meters) in length.

- The hammerhead shark gets its name from the distinctive shape of its head, which is flattened and extended into a "hammer" shape. This shape allows the shark to have a wider field of vision and to detect the electric fields of its prey.

- The poison dart frog got its name from the toxic secretions on its skin, used by indigenous people to poison the tips of their hunting darts back in the days.

- The snow leopard is a rare and elusive cat native to the mountains of central Asia. It is well equipped to live in cold and snowy environments, with thick fur and large paws that act like snowshoes.

- The platypus is a unique animal that is native to Australia. It is one of only a few mammals that lay eggs, and it has several unusual features, including a bill and webbed feet like a duck and venomous spurs on its hind legs.

- The giant anteater is a large mammal native to Central and South America. It has a long snout and a sticky tongue that it uses to feed on ants and termites.

- The mantis shrimp is a colorful and exotic species of shrimp that is known for its powerful claws, which it uses to hunt and defend itself. It is also known for its exceptional eyesight, which is thought to be the most advanced of any animal on Earth.

- The aye-aye is a type of lemur that is native to Madagascar. It is known for its long, thin middle finger, which it uses to extract insects from trees.

Chapter 19

Interesting facts about The American Revolution

- The American Revolution was fought between 1775 to 1783, a conflict between the 13 British colonies in North America, and Great Britain.

- The main motivation of the American Revolution were the colonists' desire for independence, their frustration with British taxes and regulations, and the influence of Enlightenment ideas.

- The Continental Army, which was led by George Washington, was the primary military force of the colonists during the American Revolution.

- The Declaration of Independence, adopted on July 4, 1776, declared that the 13 colonies were independent of British rule and established the United States as a new nation.

- The Battle of Saratoga, which took place in 1777, was a turning point in the American Revolution. It was a major victory for the

Continental Army and helped persuade France to enter the war on the colonists' side.

- The American Revolution was not only a military conflict but also a political and social upheaval involving significant social and cultural changes.

- The American Revolution had several important leaders, including George Washington, Benjamin Franklin, Thomas Jefferson, and John Adams.

- The Treaty of Paris, which was signed in 1783, officially ended the American Revolution and recognized the independence of the United States.

- The American Revolution had a big impact on other countries, as it inspired other movements for independence and democracy worldwide.

- The American Revolution is still remembered and celebrated in the U.S. today, with Independence Day (July 4) being a national holiday.

- One of the most famous people of the American Revolution, Paul Revere, never actually made it to the town of Concord, Massachusetts, which was his intended destination on his famous "Midnight Ride." He was captured by British soldiers before he could get there.

- The Continental Army, which fought for American independence, was made up of soldiers from all 13 colonies and was racially and ethnically diverse. There were African Americans, Native Americans, and even some foreign volunteers in its ranks.

- The British army actually burned down the White House, then known as the Presidential Mansion, during the War of 1812.

- Many people believe that the American Revolution was fought over taxation, but it was actually a complex conflict with many causes, including cultural, economic, and political differences between the colonies and Great Britain.

- During the American Revolution, the Continental Army was often short on supplies and had to resort to unconventional tactics, such as using guerrilla warfare and relying on support from the French navy.

- The Continental Congress, which was the governing body of the colonies during the American Revolution, had to constantly struggle to find ways to fund the war effort. They printed paper money, borrowed from foreign countries, and even issued bonds that could be traded like stocks.

- The Battle of Saratoga, which was a turning point in the American Revolution, was two separate battles fought several weeks apart.

- The famous "Don't Tread on Me" flag, which has become a symbol of American independence and defiance, was actually used by the Continental Navy during the American Revolution.

- The British Army used Hessian soldiers or mercenaries during the American Revolution. These soldiers were hired from the German state of Hesse-Kassel and were known for their discipline and effectiveness in battle.

- The Continental Army was made up of soldiers from all 13 colonies. In addition to fighting for their own colonies, soldiers also fought for the ideals of liberty and independence for all of the colonies.

- The Declaration of Independence wasn't signed on July 4, 1776. Most of the Founding Fathers signed the document on August 2, 1776, with a few others signing later. The first person to sign the Declaration was John Hancock, and he did so on July 4.

- Benjamin Franklin was not present at the signing of the Declaration of Independence. He was in Paris at the time, working to secure French support for the revolutionary cause.

- The first official U.S. flag was not the Stars and Stripes. The first official flag, known as the "Grand Union Flag," was flown on January 1, 1776, with the British Union Jack in the left upper corner and 13 red and white stripes symbolizing the 13 colonies.

- The Battle of Bunker Hill wasn't actually fought on Bunker Hill. Instead, the battle took place on nearby Breed's Hill, but the name "Bunker Hill" stuck because it was the original objective of the colonial forces.

- The Continental Army was not the only military force fighting for American independence. In addition to the Continental Army, state militias, naval forces, and privateers (civilians authorized by the government to attack and capture enemy ships) played important roles in the revolution.

- The British did not fight the American Revolution alone. They were aided by Native American allies, including the Mohawk leader Joseph Brant and German mercenaries known as Hessians.

- The Continental Army was often in dire need of supplies and resources. To help provide for the soldiers, the Continental Congress established a system of requisitioning or asking the states to provide a specific number of supplies and troops. However, the states were often unable or unwilling to meet these requisitions, leading to shortages and difficulties for the army.

- The Continental Army included soldiers from all different social classes, including farmers, merchants, and even enslaved people. Some slaves even fought for their freedom by joining the Continental Army, although they were not promised their freedom until after the war.

- The British army used a tactic called "scorched earth" during the American Revolution, destroying crops and buildings to weaken the Continental Army and the civilian population.

- The Continental Army was not the only group that used guerrilla tactics during the American Revolution. The British army also used these tactics, particularly in the southern colonies, where they were fighting against partisan groups.

- Desertion was a problem for both the Continental Army and the British army, with some soldiers leaving due to poor conditions, low pay, or simply a desire to return home.

- Both the Continental Army and the British army were plagued by outbreaks of diseases such as dysentery, smallpox, and typhoid fever.

- The Continental Army was not the only group to use propaganda during the American Revolution. Both sides used propaganda and misinformation to sway public opinion and win support for their cause.

- Both sides also used spies to gather intelligence and disrupt the enemy's plans.

Chapter 20

Bizarre and unbelievable facts from around the world

- In the village of Nagoro, Japan, there are more life-sized dolls than people. The dolls, made by a local artist, are placed throughout the village and used to represent the former residents who have passed away or moved away.

- In the small village of Olargues in France, all houses are painted pink. The tradition dates back to the Middle Ages when the town was required to pay a tax on the number of houses it had. To avoid paying the tax, the residents decided to paint all houses the same color, so it would appear as if only one house existed.

- In Melbourne, Australia, it is illegal to wear pink hot pants on a Sunday from midday onwards. The law, which dates back to the 1970s, is no longer enforced but is still technically on the books.

- In the small village of Dongyang in China, it is tradition for the groom's family to kidnap the bride and hold her for ransom on the wedding day. The groom's family will negotiate a price with the bride's family, and once the ransom is paid, the bride is released, and the wedding can proceed.

- In Rome, it is illegal to feed pigeons in the city center. The law, which was put in place to prevent the pigeons from causing damage to the city's historic buildings, carries a fine of up to €450.

- In the small town of Colma, California, there are more dead than living people. The town, located just south of San Francisco, is home to 17 cemeteries and only 1,200 living residents.

- In the small village of Zalipie in Poland, it is tradition for the houses and other buildings to be painted with brightly colored flowers. The tradition dates back to the 19th century when the villagers used the flowers to cover up the soot and smoke stains left by their stoves.

- In the small village of Lajedo in Brazil, it is tradition for the men to gather at the town square every Friday night and engage in a "stone throwing" competition. The men, who are all over the age of 60, compete to see who can throw a stone the farthest.

- In Reykjavik, Iceland, it used to be illegal to keep a dog as a pet. The law dates back to the 1920s and was put in place to prevent echinococcosis, a type of tapeworm, from passing from dogs to humans.

- In the small village of Sabael, New York, it is tradition for the residents to hold a "Moose Parade" every year on the 4th of July. The parade has been held annually since the late 1800s and features floats, bands, and people dressed up as moose.

- In the small village of Darsham in England, it is tradition for the villagers to gather every year on New Year's Day and roll burning tar barrels down the street. The tradition dates back to the 1800s and is believed to bring good luck to the village for the rest of the year.

- In the small village of San Juan de la Vega in Mexico, it is tradition for the villagers to participate in a "Burning of the Devil" festival every year on New Year's Eve. The festival, which has been held for over 200 years, involves burning effigies of the devil and other evil spirits to drive away bad luck.

- In the small village of Monowi, Nebraska, there is only one resident: Elsie Eiler. The village, once home to more than 150 people, has been slowly declining in population since the 1930s.

- In 2003, a man in China survived after being buried in an avalanche for six days. He was rescued when a search dog sniffed out his location.

- In 2013, a ship called the MSC Napoli was stranded off the coast of England and had to be abandoned. Local residents were caught looting the ship's cargo, which included high-end cars and luxury goods.

- In 2008, a man in India was arrested for impersonating a pilot and flying a plane for three years. He had no formal pilot training but managed to pass himself off as a qualified pilot by wearing a uniform and carrying fake documents.

- In 2010, a group of thieves stole a Degas painting worth $10 million from the Musée d'Art Moderne de la Ville de Paris. The painting was eventually recovered, but the thieves were never caught.

- In 2009, a man in Sweden discovered that he had been living with a bomb in his basement for over 50 years. The bomb, which was dropped by the Allies during World War II, was defused by bomb disposal experts.

- In 2015, a group of thieves in Brazil stole a truck full of Nutella and other chocolate products worth over $50,000. The thieves were eventually caught, but the stolen goods were never recovered.

- In 2012, a man in Egypt discovered a 3,000-year-old tomb while digging in his backyard. The tomb contained several ancient artifacts, including a mummy.

- In 2019, a group of thieves stole a gold toilet worth over $5 million from an art exhibition at Britain's Blenheim Palace. The toilet was created by the Italian artist Maurizio Cattelan.

Chapter 21

Unbelievable facts about climate change

- The Earth's temperature has increased by about 1.8 degrees Fahrenheit (1 degree Celsius) since the Industrial Revolution.

- Recycling one plastic bottle saves the energy to power a computer for 25 minutes because the process of recycling plastic uses about 70% less energy than producing plastic from raw materials.

- The measure of carbon dioxide in the atmosphere has increased by about 40% since the Industrial Revolution.

- Recycling one ton of paper saves about 7,000 gallons of water because the process of recycling paper uses less water than producing paper from raw materials.

- The most common greenhouse gas in the Earth's atmosphere is Carbon dioxide, which is responsible for about 78% of the total greenhouse effect.

- Because the Arctic ice cap is melting, the sea levels rise at a rate of about 3.2 millimeters per year.

- The Earth's oceans have absorbed about 93% of the excess heat caused by human activity.

- The average sea level has risen about 8 inches (20 centimeters) since the late 1800s globally.

- Carbon dioxide emissions from agriculture, forestry, and other land use account for about 14% of global emissions.

- The Earth's atmosphere is about 4% wetter than 100 years ago due to climate change.

- The intensity and frequency of any natural disasters, such as hurricanes and floods, have increased due to climate change.

- Carbon dioxide emissions from the residential and commercial sectors account for about 12% of global emissions.

- Recycling one ton of cardboard saves roughly 46 gallons of oil because the process of recycling cardboard uses less energy and raw materials than producing cardboard from scratch.

- The oceans are acidifying at a rate that is faster than at any time in the past 300 million years.

- Climate change is causing species extinction at a rate that is faster than at any time in the past 65 million years.

- The Earth's glaciers and ice caps are melting, causing sea levels to rise and affecting the global water cycle.

- Recycling one aluminum can saves sufficient energy to power a tv for three hours because recycling aluminum uses only about 5% of the energy required to produce aluminum from raw materials.

- Recycling one ton of paper saves the energy needed to power the average American home for six months because recycling paper uses about 60% less energy than producing paper from raw materials.

- Carbon dioxide emissions from landfills and waste incineration account for about 3% of global emissions.

- Recycling one glass bottle saves the same amount of energy needed to light a 100-watt light bulb for four hours because the process of recycling glass uses about 30% less energy than producing glass from raw materials.

- Recycling steel saves 75% of the energy required to produce steel from raw materials because the process of recycling steel uses about 75% less energy than producing steel from raw materials.

- Carbon dioxide emissions from the industrial sector account for about 21% of global emissions.

- Recycling aluminum saves 95% of the energy required to produce aluminum from raw materials because recycling aluminum uses about 95% less energy than making aluminum from raw materials.

- Carbon dioxide emissions from the extraction and use of cement account for about 5% of global emissions.

- Recycling paper saves about 60% of the energy required to produce paper from raw materials because recycling paper uses about 60% less energy than making paper from raw materials.

- Burning fossil fuel is the primary source of carbon dioxide emissions. Examples of these are coal, oil, and natural gas.

- Recycling plastic saves about 70% of the energy required to produce plastic from raw materials because recycling plastic uses about 70% less energy than producing plastic from raw materials.

- The transportation sector is the most significant contributor to carbon dioxide emissions, accounting for about 28% of global emissions.

- The electricity sector is the second-largest contributor to carbon dioxide emissions, accounting for about 25% of global emissions.

- Carbon dioxide emissions from producing iron and steel account for about 7% of global emissions.

Chapter 22

Fun facts and stories about man-made structures

- The Great Wall of China is almost 3000 years old and is the longest wall in the world. It stretches over 13,000 miles (20,921 km), visible from space, and is considered one of the world's greatest wonders.

- The Burj Khalifa in Dubai is considered the tallest man-made structure in the world, standing at over 828 meters (0.5 mile) tall. It has over 160 floors and is home to luxury apartments, hotels, and offices.

- The Eiffel Tower, located in Paris, is the most visited paid monument in the world, with over 7 million visitors yearly. It was built in 1889 for the 1889 World's Fair and was originally intended to be a temporary structure, but it has since become an iconic symbol of Paris.

- The International Space Station is the biggest man-made structure in space and has been continuously occupied by humans since 2000. It orbits around the Earth at an altitude of 250 miles (402 km) and is about the size of a football field.

- The oldest of the Seven Wonders of the Ancient World is the Great Pyramid of Giza, the only one that still stands today. It was built around 2550 BCE and is the biggest of the three pyramids in the Giza Necropolis.

- The Colosseum in Rome, also known as the Flavian Amphitheatre, is the largest amphitheater in the world. It was built in 70-80 AD and could seat up to 50,000 spectators, who would come to watch gladiator battles, animal hunts, and other forms of entertainment.

- The Sydney Opera House, located in Sydney, Australia, is a performing arts venue and is considered one of the most famous buildings worldwide. It was designed by Danish architect Jørn Utzon and was completed in 1973.

- The Golden Gate Bridge in San Francisco is a suspension bridge which spans the Golden Gate Strait, connecting San Francisco to Marin County. It is amongst the most photographed bridges worldwide and was completed in 1937.

- The Hoover Dam, a massive concrete dam on the border between Arizona and Nevada, is one of the tallest concrete dams in the world, standing at over 725 feet (221 meter) tall. It was completed in 1935 and provides power and water to several states in the southwestern United States.

- The Hoover Dam, built in the 1930s, was completed in just five years despite being a massive and complex project. Its construction required the relocation of entire towns. There are stories and legends surrounding the dam, including tales of workers being buried in its walls and secret tunnels and passageways being built into it.

- The Burj Al Arab, located in Dubai, is a luxury hotel on an artificial island off the city's coast. It is the third tallest hotel worldwide and is known for its distinctive sail-shaped design.

- The Petronas Twin Towers, located in Kuala Lumpur, Malaysia, are the tallest twin buildings worldwide, standing at 1,483 feet (452 meter) tall. They were the tallest buildings worldwide from 1998 to 2004 and are connected by a sky bridge at the 41st and 42nd floors.

- The Christ the Redeemer statue, which is found in Rio de Janeiro, Brazil, is a towering statue of Jesus Christ that stands atop the Corcovado mountain. It is among the most recognizable landmarks in the city and is listed as one of the New Seven Wonders of the World.

- The Grand Canal in Venice, Italy, is a man-made canal that runs through the city and is lined with beautiful buildings and bridges. It is one of the most famous waterways worldwide and is a popular tourist destination.

- The Suez Canal, a man-made waterway connecting the Red Sea to the Mediterranean Sea, was completed in 1869 and is an important shipping route that allows vessels to travel between Europe and Asia without going around the southern tip of Africa.

- The Leaning Tower of Pisa is a famous example of a man-made structure with a strange and humorous history. It was constructed in the 12th century and intended to be a bell tower for the Pisa Cathedral. However, it began to lean shortly after construction began due to an inadequate foundation, which has only worsened over time. Despite efforts to correct the lean, the tower has become a popular tourist attraction due to its distinctive tilt.

- The Eiffel Tower in Paris was met with great resistance when it was first proposed. Many people were against building such a large and unusual structure, and even petitions circulated to try and stop its construction. However, the tower was built for the 1889 World's Fair, and it has since become one of the most famous landmarks worldwide.

- The Great Wall of China is one of the most impressive man-made structures in the world and has a long and interesting history. It was built over many centuries to protect China from foreign invaders, and it is believed to be the only man-made structure that is visible from space. Various stories and legends surround the wall, including tales of prisoners being forced to work on its construction and workers being buried within its walls.

- The Sydney Opera House is famous worldwide for its distinctive shell-like design. Its construction was a long and difficult process and faced many challenges and setbacks. The original architect, Jørn Utzon, resigned from the project in 1966, and the building was eventually completed by other architects in 1973. Despite the difficulties, the Opera House has become among the most famous landmarks in Australia and a symbol of the city of Sydney.

- In 2008, a lightning bolt struck the Christ the Redeemer statue and damaged one of its fingers, which had to be repaired.

- The Statue of Liberty, found in New York City, is a massive copper statue on Liberty Island in New York Harbor. It was a gift from the people of France to the people of the U.S. and was completed in 1886. In 1916, a German saboteur set off a bomb in a suitcase near the statue, causing damage to the pedestal.

- The Great Sphinx of Giza is an enormous limestone statue in Egypt that depicts a sphinx. This mythical creature has a lion's body and a human or animal's head. It is thought to have been built around 2500 BCE and is amongst the oldest and most iconic monuments in the world. In 2013, a team of researchers discovered a massive void hidden within the Sphinx that may contain a secret chamber.

- The Taj Mahal, located in Agra, India, is a beautiful white marble mausoleum built by the Mughal emperor, named Shah Jahan, in memory of his wife. It is considered among the most beautiful buildings worldwide and is a UNESCO World Heritage Site. In 2007, a group of monkeys caused significant damage to the Taj Mahal when they gnawed on the electrical wires and caused a short circuit.

- The Moai statues on Easter Island are a series of massive stone statues carved by the Rapa Nui people of Easter Island. They have likely been carved between 1250 and 1500 and are amongst the most famous statues in the world. In 2011, one of the Moai statues was restored and returned to its original location after being vandalized and knocked over in the 1960s.

- The Lincoln Memorial, located in Washington, D.C., is a massive marble monument that honors Abraham Lincoln, the 16th President of the United States. It was completed in 1922 and is among the city's most visited landmarks. In 1939, singer and actor Paul Robeson gave a powerful and emotional performance of "Ol' Man River" at the Lincoln Memorial that is still remembered today.

- The Mount Rushmore National Memorial, located in South Dakota, is a massive sculpture that depicts the faces of four American presidents: George Washington, Thomas Jefferson, Abraham Lincoln, and Theodore Roosevelt. It was completed in 1941 and is amongst the most famous landmarks in the United States. In 1998, a group of activists attempted to blow up the sculpture to protest the U.S. government's treatment of Native Americans.

- The Statue of Zeus, located at Olympia in Greece, was a massive gold and ivory statue that depicted the Greek god Zeus seated on a throne. It was one of the Seven Wonders of the Ancient World, considered one of the most impressive statues of its time. In 426 AD, the statue was destroyed by a fire that swept through the temple where it was housed.

- The Colossus of Rhodes, a gigantic bronze statue that depicted the Greek sun god Helios, was one of the Seven Wonders of the Ancient World and stood over 100 feet (930 meter) tall. It was ruined in an earthquake in 226 BC, and its remains were later sold to a scrap merchant.

- The Winged Victory of Samothrace, a marble statue also known as the Victory of Samothrace, is considered among the greatest masterpieces of Hellenistic sculpture.

Chapter 23

Crazy stories about the capitals of the world

- In the early 20th century, Mexico City was sinking due to the over-extraction of underground water. To prevent further sinking, the government implemented a program to reduce water usage, which included the distribution of free condoms to encourage birth control.

- In the 1970s, Kabul, the capital of Afghanistan, was known for its laid-back atmosphere and Western influence. It was a popular destination for hippies and backpackers, who were drawn to the city's low prices and hashish.

- In the 1980s, Managua, the capital of Nicaragua, was devastated by civil war and a series of natural disasters, including an earthquake and a volcanic eruption. The city was almost completely destroyed and had to be rebuilt from scratch.

- In the 1990s, Sarajevo, the capital of Bosnia and Herzegovina, was besieged by Serbian forces during the Bosnian War. The city was subjected to daily shelling and sniper fire, and residents had to rely on underground tunnels and makeshift shelters to survive.

- In the 2000s, Baghdad, the capital of Iraq, was the site of the Iraq War and was subjected to daily bombings and attacks by insurgency groups. The city was heavily fortified and had a heavily militarized presence.

- In the 2010s, Caracas, the capital of Venezuela, was plagued by food shortages and hyperinflation, which led to widespread looting and riots. The city was also the site of numerous political protests and clashes with the police.

- In the 1980s, Washington D.C., the capital of the United States, was hit by a series of serial killings known as the "Washington D.C. Sniper Attacks." The shooters, John Allen Muhammad and Lee Boyd Malvo, killed 10 people and injured 3 others over the course of three weeks.

- In the 1970s, Tehran, the capital of Iran, was the site of the Iranian Revolution. This revolution led to the overthrow of the Shah and the establishment of an Islamic Republic. The revolution was marked by widespread protests and clashes with the police.

- In the 2000s, Phnom Penh, the capital of Cambodia, was the site of a series of bizarre crimes. Some of these included the theft of the head of a statue of Buddha and the poisoning of a pond that was home to over 100 crocodiles.

- In the 1990s, Kinshasa, the capital of the Democratic Republic of Congo, was the site of the First and Second Congo Wars, characterized by widespread atrocities and human rights abuses. The city was also home to many eccentric personalities, including a cannibal warlord known as "The Terminator."

- In the 2010s, Baghdad, the capital of Iraq, was the site of the ISIS insurgency, which led to widespread violence and the destruction of cultural heritage sites. The city was also subjected to daily bombings and attacks by the group.

- In the 2000s, Port-au-Prince, the capital of Haiti, was hit by a series of natural disasters, including a devastating earthquake in 2010 that killed over 200,000 people. The city was also the site of widespread poverty and political instability.

- In the 1990s, Mogadishu, the capital of Somalia, was the site of a civil war and the rise of the extremist group Al-Shabaab. The city was heavily damaged and was largely controlled by warlords.

- In the 1980s, Nicosia, the capital of Cyprus, was divided into a Greek-controlled southern part and a Turkish-controlled northern part by a UN-patrolled "green line." The city was a flashpoint for tensions between the two sides and was the site of frequent clashes.

- In the 1970s, Santiago, the capital of Chile, was the site of the military coup that brought dictator Augusto Pinochet to power. The city was also the site of widespread human rights abuses and political repression.

- In the 2000s, Caracas, the capital of Venezuela, was the site of a series of political protests and clashes with the government. The city was also plagued by widespread crime and violence and was home to several criminal gangs.

- In the 1990s, Port Moresby, the capital of Papua New Guinea, was the site of a series of tribal clashes known as the "PNG tribal wars." The city was also plagued by crime and was known for its high levels of HIV/AIDS.

- In the 2010s, Cairo, the capital of Egypt, was the site of the Arab Spring protests, which led to the overthrow of President Hosni Mubarak. The city was also the site of frequent clashes between protesters and the police.

- In the 2000s, Havana, the capital of Cuba, was the site of a series of political protests and clashes with the government. The city was also known for its vibrant culture and was a popular tourist destination.

- In the 1990s, Sarajevo, the capital of Bosnia and Herzegovina, was the site of the Winter Olympics, which were held during the Bosnian War. The city was heavily fortified and was protected by a heavy UN presence.

- In the 1980s, Beirut, the capital of Lebanon, was the site of a civil war that lasted for 15 years. The city was heavily bombed and was divided into rival factions controlled by different militias.

- In the 2010s, Kyiv, the capital of Ukraine, was the site of the Maidan Revolution, which led to the overthrow of President Viktor Yanukovych. The city was also the site of ongoing conflict with Russia over the annexation of Crimea.

- In the 2000s, Kabul, the capital of Afghanistan, was the site of the War in Afghanistan, fought between the Taliban and international forces. The city was heavily bombed and was the site of frequent attacks by the Taliban.

- In the 1990s, Abidjan, the capital of Côte d'Ivoire, experienced a civil war that lasted for over a decade. The city was also the site of widespread poverty and was known for its informal settlements.

- In the 1980s, Manama, the capital of Bahrain, experienced a series of political protests and clashes with the government. The city was also home to a large expatriate population and was a major financial center in the Gulf region.

Chapter 24

Interesting facts about nature

- The tallest tree on the planet is a coast redwood tree in California, which stands 379.7 feet (115.7 meters) tall.

- The longest snake on the planet is the reticulated python, reaching lengths of up to 30 feet (9 meters).

- The cheetah is the fastest land animal on the planet, and it can run at speeds of up to 75 mph (120 kph).

- The blue whale is the world's heaviest animal and weighs up to 200 tons (181 metric tons).

- The biggest flower on the planet is the Rafflesia arnoldii, which grows up to 3 feet (1 meter) in diameter and weighs up to 15 pounds (7 kilograms).

- Angel Falls in Venezuela is the tallest waterfall globally, with a total drop of 3,212 feet (979 meters).

- The Mariana Trench is considered the deepest point on Earth, located in the Pacific Ocean, and has a depth of about 36,000 feet

(10,994 meters).

- The Nile is the longest river on the planet, stretching for about 4,135 miles (6,658 kilometers) from its source in Africa to its mouth in the Mediterranean Sea.

- The largest cave in the world is the Hang Son Doong cave in Vietnam, which is over 5 miles (8 kilometers) long and has a maximum height of about 600 feet (183 meters).

- Mount Everest is the world's highest mountain above sea level, located in the Himalayas, and stands at 29,029 feet (8,848 meters) tall.

- The longest animal in the world is the lion's mane jellyfish, which can have tentacles up to 120 feet (37 meters) long.

- The giraffe is known to be the tallest mammal on Earth, reaching heights of up to 18 feet (5.5 meters).

- The largest living organism on Earth is a fungus known as Armillaria ostoyae, which covers an area of 2,200 acres (890 hectares) in Oregon, USA.

- The oldest tree worldwide is a bristlecone pine tree in California, estimated to be over 5,000 years old.

- Lake Baikal in Russia is the deepest lake on Earth, with a maximum depth of 5,387 feet (1,642 meters).

- The longest coral reef worldwide is the Great Barrier Reef in Australia, which stretches for about 1,400 miles (2,300 kilometers).

- The highest volcano in the world is Ojos del Salado in Chile, which stands at an elevation of 22,615 feet (6,893 meters).

- The Antarctic Desert is the world's largest desert, stretching about 5.5 million square miles (14.2 million square kilometers).

- The Grand Canyon in Arizona, USA, is the largest canyon in the world, which is about 277 miles (446 kilometers) long and up to 18 miles (29 kilometers) wide.

- The Mammoth Cave system in Kentucky, USA, is the longest cave system on Earth, with over 400 miles (640 kilometers) of explored passageways.

- The longest animal migration in the world is the annual migration of the wildebeest in Africa, which covers a distance of over 1,800 miles (2,900 kilometers).

- The largest living structure in the world is the Great Barrier Reef in Australia, which stretches for about 1,400 miles (2,300 kilometers).

Chapter 25

Unusual facts about kings and queens

- King Henry VIII of England had two of his wives beheaded, Anne Boleyn and Catherine Howard.

- Queen Victoria of the United Kingdom was the first known carrier of the genetic disease hemophilia, which she passed down to multiple European royal families.

- King Tutankhamun of Egypt, also known as King Tut, became Pharaoh at the age of nine and ruled for only nine years before his death at age 18.

- Queen Elizabeth II of the United Kingdom had two birthdays: her actual birthday on April 21st, and her "official" birthday, celebrated on a Saturday in June. This is because it is traditionally easier to hold outdoor celebrations for the official birthday, and the weather is more likely to be good.

- King Charles VI of France was known as "Charles the Mad" because he suffered from severe mental illness. He went through periods of psychosis, during which he believed he was made of glass and could shatter at any moment.

- Queen Elizabeth I of England was known for her love of clothes and owned over 3,000 dresses during her lifetime.

- King Ferdinand II of Aragon and Queen Isabella I of Castile financed the voyages of Christopher Columbus, which led to the discovery of the Americas.

- King Ludwig II of Bavaria was known as the "Fairy Tale King" because of his love of castles and extravagant lifestyle. He had several castles built, including the famous Neuschwanstein Castle, which inspired Disneyland's Sleeping Beauty Castle.

- Queen Nefertiti of Egypt was known for her beauty and was depicted in many paintings and sculptures with a distinctive crown and elongated neck.

- Queen Hatshepsut of Egypt was one of the few female Pharaohs in ancient Egypt and is known for her many building projects, including the construction of a temple at Deir el-Bahri.

- King Louis XVI of France suffered execution by guillotine during the French Revolution because he was found guilty of high treason by the National Convention.

- Queen Cleopatra of Egypt was known for her intelligence and beauty and was the last Pharaoh of ancient Egypt. She is also known for her relationships with Roman leaders Julius Caesar and Mark Antony.

- King George IV of the United Kingdom was known for his extravagant lifestyle and was rumored to have had a secret marriage to Catholic widow Maria Fitzherbert.

- King Olav V of Norway was a trained pilot and enjoyed flying his own plane. During World War II, he flew several missions over Norway as a liaison officer between the Norwegian government-in-exile and the Royal Air Force.

- Queen Mary I of England, also widely known as "Bloody Mary," was known for her attempts to return England to Catholicism and her persecution of Protestants.

- King James I of England was a prolific writer and is credited with authoring the King James Version of the Bible.

- The Queen Mother of the United Kingdom, Queen Elizabeth, was known for her love of cocktails and was rumored to enjoy a gin and Dubonnet before lunch every day.

- King Charles I of England was executed by beheading in 1649 after being found guilty of high treason during the English Civil War.

- King Gustav II Adolph of Sweden was a military strategist credited with helping to start the Thirty Years' War in Europe.

- Queen Anne of Great Britain, the last Stuart monarch, was known for her love of gambling and horse racing.

- King Edward VIII of the United Kingdom abdicated the throne to marry Wallis Simpson, an American socialite who was divorced twice. The Church of England, which the King was heading, did not permit the marriage of a divorced person whose former spouse was still alive. Additionally, the British government and many other royal family members opposed the marriage.

- Queen Mary II of England was the daughter of King James II. She played a crucial role in the Glorious Revolution, which overthrew her father and established a constitutional monarchy in England.

King Henry VIII of England is known for his six marriages and

- his desire to have his marriage to Catherine of Aragon annulled. When the Pope refused to grant an annulment, Henry separated from the Catholic Church and established the Church of England.

- King George III of the United Kingdom is known for his mental illness, including periods of psychosis and dementia. During one episode, he reportedly chased his wife around Windsor Castle with a knife.

- King Charles II of England is rumored to have had a secret affair with actress Nell Gwyn. When she became pregnant, Charles is said to have told her, "Pray, madam, do not wrong the Father of the Church by calling it mine."

- Queen Victoria of the United Kingdom had a tumultuous relationship with her son, Prince Edward, who later became King Edward VII. Edward was known for his love of food, as well as his fondness for women, gambling, and other forms of pleasure, a lifestyle Queen Victoria did not approve of.

- King Louis XIV of France was known for his extravagance and is said to have spent over $2 billion in today's dollars on his palace at Versailles. He is rumored to have had over 50 mistresses, including actresses and courtesans.

- Queen Elizabeth I of England is rumored to have had a secret love affair with Robert Dudley, Earl of Leicester. There were rumors that the two were engaged, but Elizabeth never married, and Dudley remained one of her closest advisors.

- King Frederick II of Prussia was known for his love of science and is credited with creating the first modern research university.

- Queen Marie Antoinette of France was known for her extravagance and is famously quoted as responding, "Let them eat cake", to the starving peasants of France. She was later executed by guillotine during the French Revolution.

- Queen Elizabeth II, the longest-reigning British monarch, was also an accomplished equestrian and has ridden horses since childhood.

Chapter 26

Food and drinks around the world

- The world's oldest known fruitcake was found in an Egyptian tomb and is over 3000 years old.

- The world's hottest pepper is the Carolina Reaper, which can measure over 2 million Scoville heat units (a measure of spiciness). By comparison, a jalapeno pepper measures between 2,500 and 8,000 Scoville heat units.

- The world's largest cupcake weighed over 2000 pounds (907 kg) and was nearly 8 feet (2.4 meters) tall.

- The world's most expensive coffee is made from beans that have been eaten by civets (small mammals), partially digested, and then defecated. The coffee is called Kopi Luwak and can cost over $100 per pound (0.45 kg).

- The world's largest pizza was over 122 feet (37 meters) in diameter and was made in Rome, Italy, in 2012.

- The world's largest ice cream sundae weighed over 50 tons and was made in Edmonton, Alberta, Canada, in 1988.

- The white truffle is the world's most expensive edible mushroom, costing over $1000 per pound (0.45 kg).

- The world's oldest known recipe for beer is believed to be over 4,000 years old and comes from ancient Sumeria (present-day southern Iraq). The recipe is inscribed on a clay tablet and was written in cuneiform script.

- The world's most giant bowl of cereal was created on September 27, 2014, in Battle Creek, Michigan, USA. The cereal bowl was made by Kellogg's, a famous cereal company, and filled with over 44,000 pounds (20,000 kg) of cereal. The bowl was 12 feet (3.7 meters) wide, 6 feet (1.8 meters) tall, and 8 feet (2.4 meters) deep. The event was organized to celebrate Kellogg's 110th anniversary and to raise awareness and funds for the United Way charity organization.

- The world's longest sausage was over a mile (1.6 km) long and was made in Germany in 2013.

- The world's most giant smoothie weighed over 500 pounds (227 kg) and was made in Dubai in 2012.

- The world's largest gumbo was made in Louisiana in 2010 by a group of volunteers in New Iberia. The gumbo weighed over 10,000 pounds (4,536 kg) and was cooked in a pot over 20 feet (6 meters) wide. It was made with chicken, sausage, seafood, and vegetables and served to thousands of people at the annual Gumbo Cook-Off.

- The world's most enormous omelet weighed over 145 pounds (66 kg) and was made in France in 2011.

- The world's most giant pumpkin pie weighed over 350 pounds (159 kg) and was made in New York in 2010.

- The world's largest ice cream sundae was over 120 feet (37 Meters) long and was made in California in 1991.

- The world's largest gingerbread house was built in Bryan, Texas, USA, in 2013. The gingerbread house measured 60 foot by 42 foot (18.3meters by 12.8meters) and was made using over a million pounds (over 450,000 kg) of gingerbread, icing, and candy. The house was built on the grounds of the Traditions Club, a private golf and country club, and it was open to the public for tours and events during the holiday season. The construction of the house took over a month, and it was made with the help of local community members, including students from Texas A&M University, who helped create and decorate the gingerbread.

- The world's most giant sushi roll was created by a group of sushi chefs in Los Angeles, California, USA, in 2016. The roll was made with traditional sushi ingredients such as rice, seaweed, fish, and vegetables. It weighed over 2,000 pounds (907 kg) and measured over 2,000 feet (609 meters) in length. The roll was made using traditional sushi-making techniques and modern technology.

- The world's most expensive cocktail is called the "Ruby Rose" and is served at the Ritz-Carlton in Tokyo. It is made with a rare cognac that costs over $26,000 per bottle and is garnished with a 1-carat ruby. The cocktail costs over $17,000.

- The world's largest cocktail was over 10,000 gallons (over 37,000 liters) and was made in Las Vegas in 2011.

- The world's strongest coffee, called "Black Insomnia, " has over 700 milligrams of caffeine per 12 ounces. By comparison, a typical cup of coffee has around 100 milligrams of caffeine.

- The world's largest wine bottle was over 26 feet (7.9 meters) tall and held over 100,000 bottles of wine. It was made in France in

2012.

- The world's largest margarita weighed over 500 pounds (227 kg) and was made in Texas in 2012.

- The world's largest cup of coffee was over 100,000 gallons (378,541 liters) and was made in Italy in 2010.

- In Sweden, a popular type of candy is "Lakrits", made from licorice root and known for its strong, earthy flavor.

- Kit Kat Sake is a unique type of sake made by infusing the sake with the flavor of the chocolate, resulting in a sweet and unique taste. The flavor of the Kit Kat chocolate is said to complement the taste of the sake, creating a balance between the sweetness and the alcohol.

- In China, a popular dish is "Stinky Tofu", which is fermented tofu that has a strong, pungent odor.

- In Vietnam, a popular dish is "Balut," a fertilized duck egg that has been incubated for several weeks and then boiled.

- In Italy, a popular dish is "Casu Marzu," a cheese made with live insect larvae.

- In Japan, it is not uncommon to eat raw horse meat, known as "basashi." It is often served thinly sliced and accompanied by soy sauce and grated ginger.

- In certain parts of China, people eat live baby mice, which are believed to have medicinal properties.

- In Thailand, a popular snack called "insect kabobs" can be found at street markets. These skewers are typically grilled and feature a variety of insects, such as beetles, grasshoppers, and worms.

- It is not uncommon to find "witchetty grubs" on the menu in Australia. These are the larval form of a type of moth and are typically eaten roasted or as part of a traditional Aboriginal stew.

- In the Philippines, a dish called "balut" is made with fertilized duck eggs that are boiled and eaten while still in the shell. The eggs contain partially developed duck embryos, which are considered a delicacy.

- In Scandinavia, a popular Christmas treat called "lutefisk" is made with dried, salted cod that has been soaked in lye for several days. It is then boiled and often served with potatoes and a white sauce.

- In Peru, a popular drink called "chicha" is made by chewing corn and spitting it into a container. It ferments for several days, and the beverage is sweet and slightly sour.

- In Russia, a traditional drink called "kvass" is made from fermented bread or grain. It is often flavored with fruit or herbs and has a slightly sour taste.

- In Turkey, a drink called "ayran" is made with yogurt, water, and salt. It is typically served cold and is very refreshing on a hot day.

- In Vietnam, a drink called "nuoc mia" is made by pressing sugar cane through a machine to extract the juice. It is often served over ice and can be flavored with lime or other fruit juices.

Chapter 27

Interesting facts about America from the 1950s

- The United States experienced a baby boom in the 1950s, with the birth rate reaching an all-time high in 1957.

- In 1950, the United States became involved in the Korean War, a conflict between North and South Korea that lasted until 1953 and resulted in the deaths of over 33,000 U.S. soldiers.

- The 1950s saw the emergence of the rockabilly movement, with artists like Elvis Presley and Johnny Cash becoming popular.

- The United States experienced a "red scare" in the 1950s, characterized by a fear of communist infiltration and the blacklisting of suspected communists in the entertainment industry.

- The science fiction genre became popular in the 1950s with the release of films like "The War of the Worlds" and "The Day the Earth Stood Still."

- The United States experienced a polio epidemic in the 1950s, with over 21,000 cases reported in 1952 alone. The arrival of the polio vaccine in 1955 helped to bring the outbreak under control.

- The 1950s saw the rise of the television industry, with the first Emmy Awards being held in 1949.

- In 1954, the U.S. Supreme Court ruled in Brown v. Board of Education that segregation in public schools was unconstitutional, leading to the civil rights movement.

- The United States and the Soviet Union competed in a "space race" in the 1950s, with the Soviet Union launching the first successful satellite, Sputnik, in 1957 and the United States launching the first successful manned mission, Mercury, in 1961.

- The 1950s saw the rise of rock and roll music, with artists like Elvis Presley and Chuck Berry becoming popular.

- The United States experienced a wave of UFO sightings in the 1950s, including the famous "Roswell Incident," in which the U.S. military claimed to have recovered a crashed flying saucer.

- The first successful kidney transplant took place in the United States in 1950.

- The United States experienced a series of natural disasters in the 1950s, including the 1952 Los Angeles smog disaster and the 1957 Hurricane Audrey, which caused over 500 deaths in Texas and Louisiana.

- In 1952, the United States tested its first hydrogen bomb, which was 1000 times more powerful than the atomic bomb dropped on Hiroshima.

The 1950s saw the emergence of the civil rights movement, with

- key events like the Montgomery Bus Boycott and the Greensboro sit-ins.

- The 1950s saw the rise of the Cold War, with tensions between the United States and the Soviet Union leading to a period of political and military tension.

- The feminist movement emerged in the 1950s with the growth of organizations like the National Organization for Women and the Women's Strike for Peace.

- The 1950s saw the rise of consumer culture, with the proliferation of credit and the emergence of the suburban lifestyle.

- The blues rock movement emerged in the 1950s, with artists like Muddy Waters and B.B. King becoming popular.

- The 1950s saw the rise of the teen movie genre, with films like "Rebel Without a Cause" and "Grease" becoming popular.

- The country music movement emerged in the 1950s, with artists like Hank Williams and Johnny Cash becoming popular.

- The horror movie genre became popular in the 1950s, with films like "The Thing from Another World" and "The Blob" being released.

- The 1950s saw the emergence of the jazz-rock movement, with artists like Miles Davis and John Coltrane becoming popular.

- The computer game industry rose in popularity in the 1950s, with the release of the first computer game, "Tennis for Two," in 1958.

Chapter 28

Interesting facts about America from the 1960s

- The population of the United States in the 1960s was approximately 180 million people.

- In the 1960s, the United States experienced significant social and political changes, including civil rights, anti-war, and counter-culture movements. Protests against the Vietnam War became increasingly common.

- The first Super Bowl, known as the "AFL-NFL World Championship Game," was played in January 1967.

- The 1960s saw the emergence of the feminist movement, with the growth of organizations like the National Organization for Women and the Women's Strike for Peace.

- The first-ever manned moon landing occurred on July 20, 1969, when NASA's Apollo 11 mission successfully landed on the moon.

- The 1960s saw the rise of popular music genres such as rock and roll, soul, and surf music. Some of the decade's most popular bands and artists included the Beatles, the Rolling Stones, and the Beach Boys.

- The first Walmart store opened its doors in Rogers, Arkansas, in 1962.

- The 1960s saw the rise of the civil rights movement, with key events like the Civil Rights Act of 1964 and the Voting Rights Act of 1965 leading to significant changes in how minority groups were treated in the United States.

- The 1960s saw the rise of the environmental movement, with the creation of organizations like Earth Day and the Sierra Club.

- The first installment of the Star Trek television series aired in September 1966.

- In 1963, Douglas Engelbart invented the first-ever computer mouse.

- The mini skirt, which became a symbol of the sexual revolution, became popular in the 1960s.

- There was a shortage of grave sites in the United States in the 1960s due to the high number of deaths caused by the Vietnam War and the HIV/AIDS epidemic.

- The Central Intelligence Agency (CIA) conducted secret experiments on unsuspecting Americans, including the administration of LSD to military personnel and civilians.

- The Ku Klux Klan, which was a white supremacist organization, saw a resurgence in membership in the 1960s, with a peak of around 4 million members.

- The 1960s saw the rise of the gay rights movement, with the formation of the Mattachine Society and the Daughters of Bilitis.

- There were several assassination attempts on public figures in the 1960s, including President John F. Kennedy in 1963 and civil rights leader Martin Luther King Jr. in 1968.

- The 1960s saw the rise of the "hippie" counterculture, characterized by the use of drugs, rejection of mainstream values, and experimentation with alternative lifestyles.

- The 1960s saw the rise of the youth movement, with young people becoming more politically active and advocating for social change.

- The first heart transplant took place in the United States in 1967.

- In 1969, Native American activists, including members of the Mohawk tribe, occupied Alcatraz Island in San Francisco Bay to protest the federal government's treatment of Native Americans.

- The "Zodiac Killer", a serial killer operating in Northern California in the late 1960s and early 1970s, was never caught, and the criminal case remains unsolved.

- The 1960s saw the rise of the psychedelic drug movement, with the popularity of drugs like LSD and psilocybin.

- In 1968, U.S. athletes John Carlos and Tommie Smith raised their fists in protest during the medal ceremony at the Summer Olympics in Mexico City, causing controversy and resulting in their suspension from the U.S. Olympic team.

- In the 1960s, the United States went through a series of natural disasters, including the 1962 Columbus Day Storm, which was the strongest Pacific Northwest windstorm on record, and the 1964 Alaska earthquake, which was the largest earthquake in U.S. history.

- The 1960s saw the emergence of the peace movement, with the growth of organizations like the Peace Corps and Peace Action.

- The U.S. government conducted secret experiments on the effects of radiation on human subjects, including the "Marshall Islands Project," in which U.S. servicemen were exposed to radioactive fallout from nuclear weapon tests.

- The first human space flight took place in 1961 when NASA astronaut Alan Shepard became the first American to be launched into space.

- The first U.S. military draft lottery since World War II was held in December 1969, determining the order in which young men would be enrolled to serve in the Vietnam War.

- The United States experienced a series of race riots in the 1960s, including the Watts Riots in Los Angeles in 1965 and the Detroit Riots in 1967.

- In 1964, the Civil Rights Act was signed into law, prohibiting discrimination based on race, color, religion, sex, or national origin and ensuring voting rights for African Americans, respectively. Still, it was not until the Fair Housing Act of 1968 that housing discrimination was also made illegal.

- The first heart-lung transplant was performed in the United States in 1981.

- The U.S. Surgeon General released a report in 1964 warning that smoking causes lung cancer, leading to significant changes in public attitudes towards smoking.

- The 1960s saw the rise of the psychedelic drug movement, with the popularity of drugs like LSD and psilocybin.

- The United States and the Soviet Union neared a nuclear war during the Cuban Missile Crisis in 1962, a 13-day confrontation between the two superpowers over the Soviet Union's installation of nuclear missiles in Cuba.

- The Stonewall Riots in New York City in 1969 is considered a turning point in the modern gay rights movement. These riots were a series of protests by the LGBTQ+ community against a police raid on the Stonewall Inn.

- The U.S. government conducted secret experiments on the effects of psychoactive drugs on soldiers and civilians, including the "MKUltra" project, in which people were given drugs without their knowledge or consent.

- The 1960s saw the rise of the counterculture movement, with the growth of the hippie movement and the popularity of the counterculture lifestyle.

- President John F. Kennedy was assassinated in Dallas, Texas, in 1963, leading to widespread grief and shock.

- The 1960s saw the emergence of the Black Power movement, with the growth of organizations like the Black Panther Party.

- The 1960s saw the emergence of the free speech movement, with the growth of organizations like the Student Nonviolent Coordinating Committee.

- In 1964, the Warren Commission released its report on President John F. Kennedy's assassination, concluding that Lee Harvey Oswald acted alone.

- The 1960s saw the rise of the youth culture, with bands like The Beatles and The Rolling Stones becoming popular and the emergence of youth-oriented fashion and music.

Chapter 29

Interesting facts about America from the 1970s

- The 1970s saw disco music rise in popularity and the popularization of dance clubs. The song "Stayin' Alive" by the Bee Gees and the movie "Saturday Night Fever" helped to popularize the genre.

- In 1971, the 26th Amendment to the United States Constitution was ratified, which lowered the voting age from 21 to 18.

- The first Earth Day took place on April 22, 1970.

- Some of the highest-grossing films ever were released in the 1970s, including "Jaws," "Star Wars," and "The Godfather."

- The 1970s saw the rise of the gay rights movement, with the growth of organizations like the Gay Liberation Front and the Gay Activists Alliance.

- The Watergate scandal, resulting in the resignation of President Richard Nixon, dominated headlines in the 1970s.

- The 1970s saw the emergence of punk rock music, with bands like the Ramones and the Sex Pistols leading the movement.

- The first personal computer, the Altair 8800, was released in 1975.

- In 1977, the first ever Star Wars movie was released and became a cultural phenomenon.

- The first mobile phone call took place in 1971, but it wasn't until the late 1970s that cellular technology became widely available.

- The 1970s saw the rise of the "me generation," as people focused on personal growth and development.

- In 1976, the first Apple computer was released.

- The 1970s saw the emergence of the feminist movement and the fight for women's rights.

- The 1970s saw the rise of the environmental movement, with the creation of organizations like Greenpeace and the Sierra Club.

- The 1970s saw the rise of hip-hop music, with the release of the first rap record, "Rapper's Delight" by The Sugarhill Gang, in 1979.

- The 1970s saw the rise of the video game industry with the release of the Atari 2600 in 1977.

- The 1970s saw the counterculture movement emerge with the growth of communes and the popularity of the hippie lifestyle.

- The 1970s saw the rise of the women's liberation movement, with the growth of feminist organizations and the push for equal rights for women.

- The punk rock movement emerged in the 1970s, with the growth of punk rock bands and the popularity of the punk lifestyle.

Chapter 30

Interesting facts about America from the 1980s

- In 1981, the first space shuttle, the Columbia, was launched.

- The 1980s saw the rise of pop culture icons like Madonna and Michael Jackson and the emergence of music videos as a popular medium.

- In the 1980s, the personal computer rose in popularity, with the release of the IBM PC in 1981 and later the Apple Macintosh in 1984.

- In 1985, the first .com domain was registered, marking the beginning of the internet as we know it today.

- The 1980s saw the rise of the fitness craze, with the release of Jane Fonda's workout video in 1982 and the popularity of aerobic exercise.

- The hip-hop movement rose in the 1980s, with the release of the first rap record, "Rapper's Delight" by The Sugarhill Gang, in 1979.

- The 1980s saw the rise of the video game industry with the release of the Nintendo Entertainment System in 1985.

- In 1986, the Space Shuttle Challenger tragedy occurred, resulting in the deaths of seven astronauts.

- The environmental movement emerged in the 1980s with the creation of organizations like Greenpeace and the Sierra Club.

- The 1980s saw the rise of the glam metal movement, with bands like Mötley Crüe and Guns N' Roses leading the way.

- The alternative rock movement started in the 1980s, and bands like R.E.M. and The Smiths led the way.

- The 1980s saw the rise of the teen movie genre, with films like "The Breakfast Club" and "Ferris Bueller's Day Off" becoming popular.

- The 1980s saw the rise of the hair metal movement, with bands like Poison and Cinderella leading the way.

- The grunge movement emerged in the 1980s, with bands like Nirvana and Pearl Jam leading the way.

Chapter 31

Interesting facts about America from the 1990s

- In 1993, the World Wide Web was made available to the general public, marking a major milestone in the development of the internet.

- The 1990s saw the rise of boy bands and girl groups, with groups like NSYNC and The Spice Girls becoming popular.

- The 1990s saw the emergence of the grunge movement, with bands like Nirvana and Pearl Jam leading the way.

- The 1990s saw the rise of the alternative rock movement, with bands like Radiohead and Weezer becoming popular.

- The 1990s saw the rise of the hip-hop movement, with artists like Tupac Shakur and Notorious B.I.G. becoming popular.

- The 1990s saw the rise of the computer animation industry, with the release of the first fully computer-animated feature film, "Toy

Story," in 1995.

- The 1990s saw the emergence of the reality TV genre, with shows like "Survivor" and "The Real World" becoming popular.

- The 1990s saw the rise of the teen movie genre, with films like "Clueless" and "Scream" becoming popular.

- The 1990s saw the emergence of the electronic dance music movement, with the popularity of genres like techno and house music.

- The 1990s saw the rise of the fantasy movie genre with the release of the "Harry Potter" and "Lord of the Rings" film series.

Chapter 32

Interesting facts about America from the 2000s

- In 2000, the United States presidential election between George W. Bush and Al Gore ended in controversy and was ultimately decided by the Supreme Court.

- The 2000s saw the rise of reality TV, with shows like "American Idol" and "Survivor" becoming popular.

- The 2000s saw the emergence of social media with the launch of platforms like Facebook and Twitter.

- iPod and other portable music devices rose in popularity during the 2000s, leading to a decline in CD sales.

- The 2000s saw the emergence of the indie rock movement, with bands like The Strokes and The White Stripes becoming popular.

- The 2000s saw the rise of the superhero movie and TV genre with the release of films like "Spider-Man" and "The Dark Knight" and

TV shows like "Smallville" and "Heroes".

- The 2000s saw the emergence of the emo movement, with bands like Fall Out Boy and My Chemical Romance becoming popular.

- The 2000s saw the rise of the fantasy book and movie genre with the release of the "Harry Potter" and "Lord of the Rings" film series.

- The 2000s saw the emergence of the electronic dance music movement, with the popularity of genres like techno and house music.

- The first iPhone was released in 2007, contributing to the rise of the smartphone in the 2000s.

- The 2000s saw the rise of the hip-hop movement, with artists like Kanye West and Jay-Z becoming popular.

- The teen movie genre, with films like "Mean Girls" and "The Hunger Games", became popular during the 2000s.

- The 2000s saw the emergence of the indie pop movement, with bands like Vampire Weekend and The Strokes becoming popular.

- The computer game industry rose throughout the 2000s, with the release of popular games like "World of Warcraft" and "Call of Duty."

- The 2000s saw the emergence of the punk rock movement, with bands like Green Day and Blink-182 becoming popular.

- The 2000s saw the emergence of the emo-pop movement, with bands like Panic! at the Disco and Fall Out Boy becoming popular.

- The 2000s saw the emergence of the indie folk movement, with bands like Bon Iver and Fleet Foxes becoming popular.

- The 2000s saw the emergence of the electronic music movement, with the popularity of genres like EDM and techno.

Chapter 33

Interesting facts about America from the 2010s

- The 2010s saw the emergence of social media influencers, with individuals gaining large followings on platforms like Instagram and YouTube.

- In 2011, the United States conducted a military operation resulting in Osama bin Laden's death, the leader of the terrorist group Al-Qaeda.

- Streaming platforms like Netflix and Hulu rose in popularity in the 2010s, leading to a decline in traditional cable TV subscriptions.

- The 2010s saw the smartphone rise in popularity after the first iPhone's release in 2007 and the increase in the popularity of Android devices.

- The 2010s saw the rise in the hip-hop movement, with artists like Kendrick Lamar and Drake becoming popular.

- The 2010s saw the rise of the superhero movie genre, with the release of films like "The Avengers" and "Black Panther."

- The 2010s saw the emergence of the indie rock movement, with bands like The 1975 and Tame Impala becoming popular.

- The 2010s saw the rise of the fantasy movie genre with the release of the "Harry Potter" and "The Hunger Games" film series.

- The 2010s saw the rise of the electronic dance music movement, with the popularity of genres like techno and house music.

- The 2010s saw the rise of the computer game industry with the release of popular games like "Fortnite" and "Minecraft."

- The 2010s saw the emergence of the indie pop movement, with bands like Vampire Weekend and The Strokes becoming popular.

- The 2010s saw the rise of the teen movie genre, with films like "The Fault in Our Stars" and "The Maze Runner" becoming popular.

- The 2010s saw the emergence of the emo-pop movement, with bands like Panic! at the Disco and Fall Out Boy becoming popular.

- The 2010s saw the rise of the fantasy book genre with the release of the "Harry Potter" and "The Hunger Games" series.

- The 2010s saw the rise of the indie folk movement, with bands like Bon Iver and Fleet Foxes becoming popular.

- The 2010s saw the rise of the superhero TV show genre with the release of shows like "The Flash" and "Arrow."

- The 2010s saw the rise of the electronic music movement, with the popularity of genres like EDM and techno.

- The 2010s saw the rise of the streaming music industry with the launch of platforms like Spotify and Apple Music.

Made in United States
Orlando, FL
05 May 2023

32820678R00085